The Ukulele playlist

Folk

© 2013 by Faber Music Ltd
First published in 2013 by Faber Music Ltd
Bloomsbury House
74–77 Great Russell Street
London WC1B 3DA

Arranged by Alex Davis
Edited by Lucy Holliday

Designed by Sue Clarke
Photography by Ben Turner

Printed in England by Caligraving Ltd
All rights reserved

ISBN10: 0-571-53831-2
EAN13: 978-0-571-53831-7

buy Faber Music publications or to find out about
e full range of titles available, please contact your
ocal music retailer or Faber Music sales enquiries:

Faber Music Ltd, Burnt Mill, Elizabeth Way,
Harlow, CM20 2HX England

Tel: +44(0)1279 82 89 82
Fax: +44(0)1279 82 89 83

sales@fabermusic.com
fabermusicstore.com

Tuning

The standard Ukulele string tuning is G–C–E–A, shown here on the treble stave and piano keyboard. Note that the G string is tuned higher than the C string.

You can tune your Ukulele using a piano or keyboard (or any other instrument that you know is in tune!) or by using an electronic chromatic tuner.

If just one string on your Ukulele is in tune then you can use it to tune the other strings as well.

This diagram shows which fretted notes match the note of the open string above. Eg. Pluck the first string at the 5th fret and match the note to the second open string, and so on.

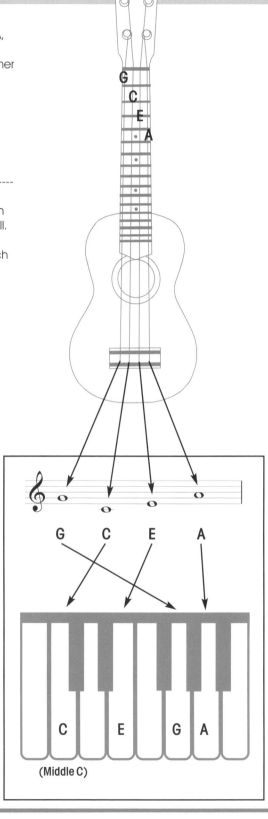

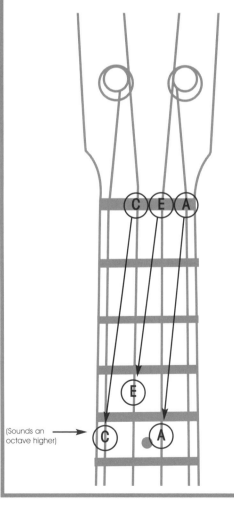

(Sounds an octave higher)

(Middle C)

Reading Chord Boxes

A chord box is basically a diagram of how a chord is played on the neck of the Ukulele. It shows you which string to play, where to put your fingers and whereabouts on the neck the chord is played.

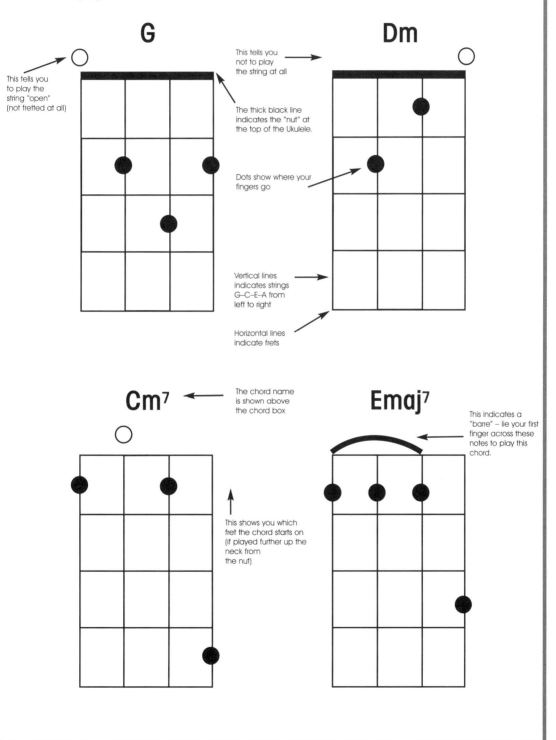

This tells you to play the string "open" (not fretted at all)

This tells you not to play the string at all

The thick black line indicates the "nut" at the top of the Ukulele.

Dots show where your fingers go

Vertical lines indicates strings G–C–E–A from left to right

Horizontal lines indicate frets

The chord name is shown above the chord box

This shows you which fret the chord starts on (if played further up the neck from the nut)

This indicates a "barre" – lie your first finger across these notes to play this chord.

Barbara Allen

Words and Music Traditional

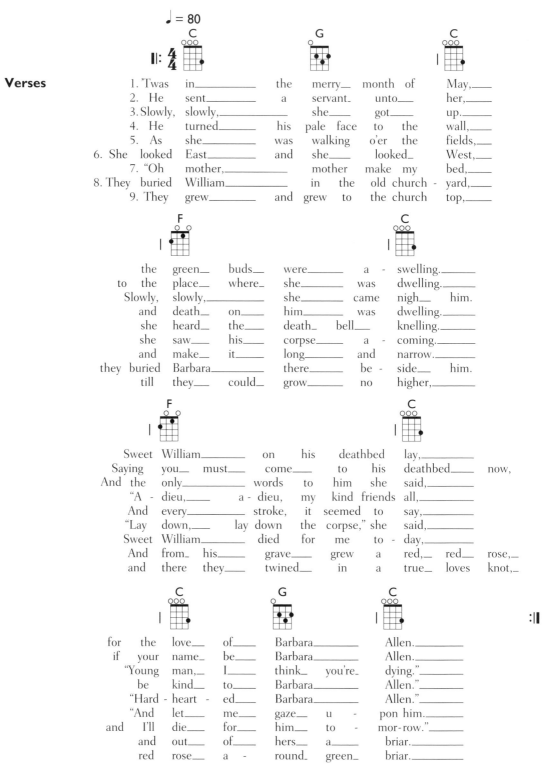

Verses

♩ = 80

C · G · C

1. 'Twas   in   the   merry month of   May,
2. He   sent   a   servant unto her,
3. Slowly, slowly,   she got up.
4. He   turned   his   pale face   to   the   wall,
5. As   she   was   walking   o'er   the   fields,
6. She looked East   and   she looked West,
7. "Oh   mother,   mother make my bed,
8. They buried William   in   the   old church - yard,
9. They   grew   and grew to   the church   top,

F · C

the   green buds were a - swelling.
to   the   place where she was   dwelling.
Slowly,   slowly, she came   nigh him.
and   death on him was   dwelling.
she   heard the death bell knelling.
she   saw his corpse a - coming.
and   make it long and   narrow.
they buried Barbara there be - side him.
till   they could grow no   higher,

F · C

Sweet William on   his   deathbed   lay,
Saying   you must come to   his   deathbed now,
And   the   only words   to   him   she   said,
"A - dieu, a - dieu,   my   kind friends   all,
And   every stroke,   it   seemed   to   say,
"Lay   down, lay down   the   corpse,"   she   said,
Sweet William died   for   me   to - day,
And   from his grave grew   a   red, red rose,
and   there   they twined in   a   true loves   knot,

C · G · C

for   the   love of Barbara Allen.
if   your   name be Barbara Allen.
"Young   man, I think you're dying."
be   kind to Barbara Allen."
"Hard - heart - ed Barbara Allen."
"And   let me gaze u - pon him.
and   I'll   die for him to - mor-row."
and   out of hers a briar.
red   rose a - round green briar.

The Boar's Head Carol

Words and Music Traditional

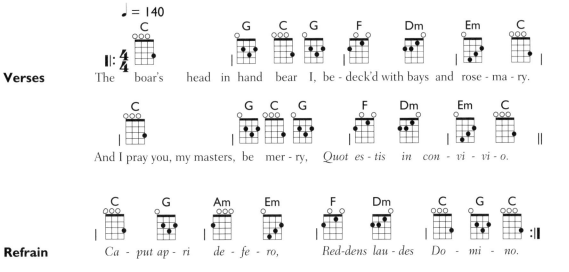

Verses The boar's head in hand bear I, be - deck'd with bays and rose - ma - ry.

And I pray you, my masters, be mer - ry, *Quot es - tis in con - vi - vi - o.*

Refrain *Ca - put ap - ri de - fe - ro, Red-dens lau - des Do - mi - no.*

Verse 2:

The boar's head, as I understand
Is the bravest dish in all the land
When thus bedeck'd with a gay garland
Let us *servire cantico*

Verse 3:

Our steward hath provided this
In honour of the King of Bliss
Which on this day to be served is
In *Reginensi Atrio*

Cockles And Mussels

Words and Music Traditional

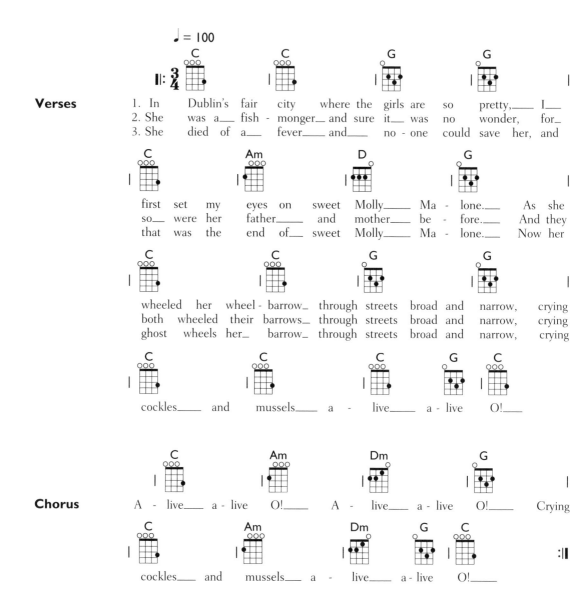

Verses

♩ = 100

| C | C | G | G |

1. In Dublin's fair city where the girls are so pretty,___ I___
2. She was a___ fish - monger___ and sure it___ was no wonder, for___
3. She died of a___ fever___ and___ no - one could save her, and

| C | Am | D | G |

first set my eyes on sweet Molly___ Ma - lone.___ As she
so___ were her father___ and mother___ be - fore.___ And they
that was the end of___ sweet Molly___ Ma - lone.___ Now her

| C | C | G | G |

wheeled her wheel - barrow___ through streets broad and narrow, crying
both wheeled their barrows___ through streets broad and narrow, crying
ghost wheels her___ barrow___ through streets broad and narrow, crying

| C | C | C | G | C |

cockles___ and mussels___ a - live___ a - live O!___

Chorus

| C | Am | Dm | G |

A - live___ a - live O!___ A - live___ a - live O!___ Crying

| C | Am | Dm | G | C |

cockles___ and mussels___ a - live___ a - live O!___

Come All You Fair And Tender Ladies

Words and Music Traditional

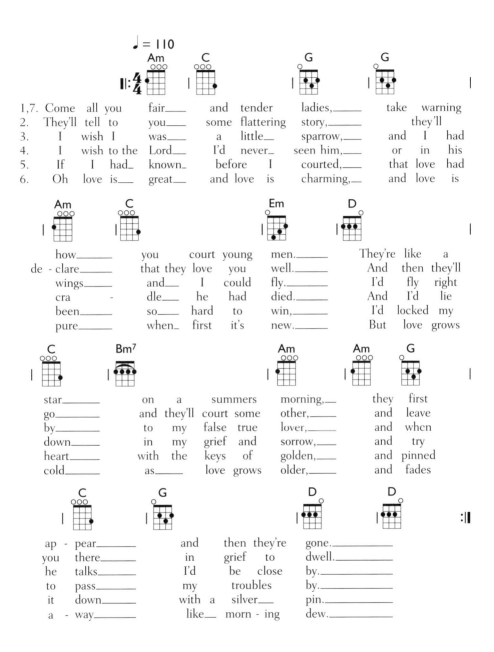

Verses

1,7. Come all you fair___ and tender ladies,___ take warning
2. They'll tell to you___ some flattering story,___ they'll
3. I wish I was___ a little__ sparrow,___ and I had
4. I wish to the Lord___ I'd never_ seen him,___ or in his
5. If I had_ known_ before I courted,___ that love had
6. Oh love is__ great___ and love is charming,__ and love is

how_____ you court young men._____ They're like a
de - clare_____ that they love you well._____ And then they'll
wings_____ and__ I could fly._____ I'd fly right
cra - dle__ he had died._____ And I'd lie
been_____ so___ hard to win,_____ I'd locked my
pure_____ when_ first it's new.____ But love grows

star_____ on a summers morning,__ they first
go_____ and they'll court some other,_____ and leave
by_____ to my false true lover,_____ and when
down____ in my grief and sorrow,___ and try
heart____ with the keys of golden,___ and pinned
cold_____ as___ love grows older,_____ and fades

ap - pear_____ and then they're gone._____
you there_____ in grief to dwell._____
he talks_____ I'd be close by._____
to pass_____ my troubles by._____
it down_____ with a silver_ pin._____
a - way_____ like_ morn - ing dew._____

Danny Boy

Words and Music Traditional

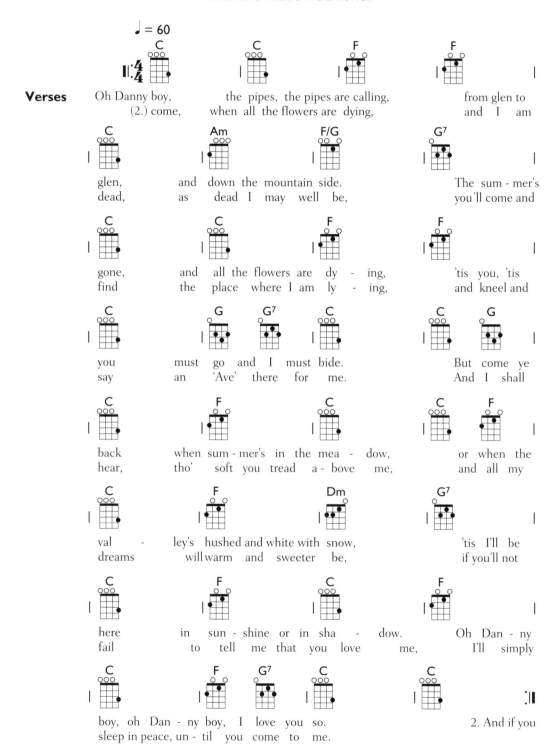

♩ = 60

Verses

Oh Danny boy,   the pipes, the pipes are calling,   from glen to
(2.) come,   when all the flowers are dying,   and I am

glen,   and down the mountain side.   The sum - mer's
dead,   as dead I may well be,   you'll come and

gone,   and all the flowers are dy - ing,   'tis you, 'tis
find   the place where I am ly - ing,   and kneel and

you   must go and I must bide.   But come ye
say   an 'Ave' there for me.   And I shall

back   when sum - mer's in the mea - dow,   or when the
hear,   tho' soft you tread a - bove me,   and all my

val -   ley's hushed and white with snow,   'tis I'll be
dreams   will warm and sweeter be,   if you'll not

here   in sun - shine or in sha - dow.   Oh Dan - ny
fail   to tell me that you love me,   I'll simply

boy, oh Dan - ny boy, I love you so.   2. And if you
sleep in peace, un - til you come to me.

Down By The Salley Gardens

Words and Music Traditional

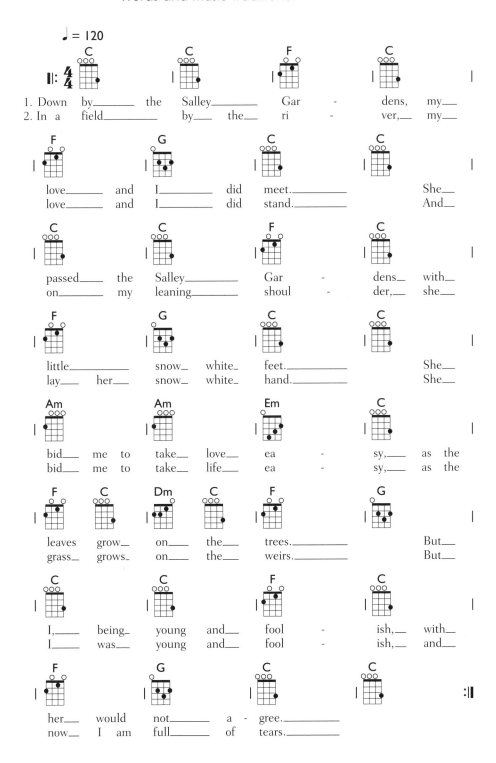

Verses

1. Down by the Salley Gar - dens, my love and I did meet. She passed the Salley Gar - dens with little snow white feet. She bid me to take love ea - sy, as the leaves grow on the trees. But I, being young and fool - ish, with her would not a - gree.

2. In a field by the ri - ver, my love and I did stand. And on my leaning shoul - der, she lay her snow white hand. She bid me to take life ea - sy, as the grass grows on the weirs. But I was young and fool - ish, and now I am full of tears.

Early One Morning

Words and Music Traditional

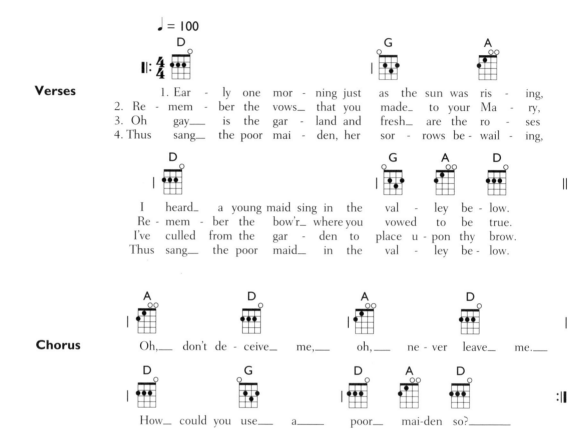

♩ = 100

Verses

D   G   A

1. Ear - ly one mor - ning just as the sun was ris - ing,
2. Re - mem - ber the vows_ that you made_ to your Ma - ry,
3. Oh gay_ is the gar - land and fresh_ are the ro - ses
4. Thus sang_ the poor mai - den, her sor - rows be - wail - ing,

D   G   A   D

I heard_ a young maid sing in the val - ley be - low.
Re - mem - ber the bow'r_ where you vowed to be true.
I've culled from the gar - den to place u - pon thy brow.
Thus sang_ the poor maid_ in the val - ley be - low.

Chorus

A   D   A   D

Oh,_ don't de - ceive_ me,_ oh, _ ne - ver leave_ me._

D   G   D   A   D

How_ could you use_ a_ poor_ mai-den so?_

Fakenham Fair
Words and Music Traditional
Arranged by Jon Boden

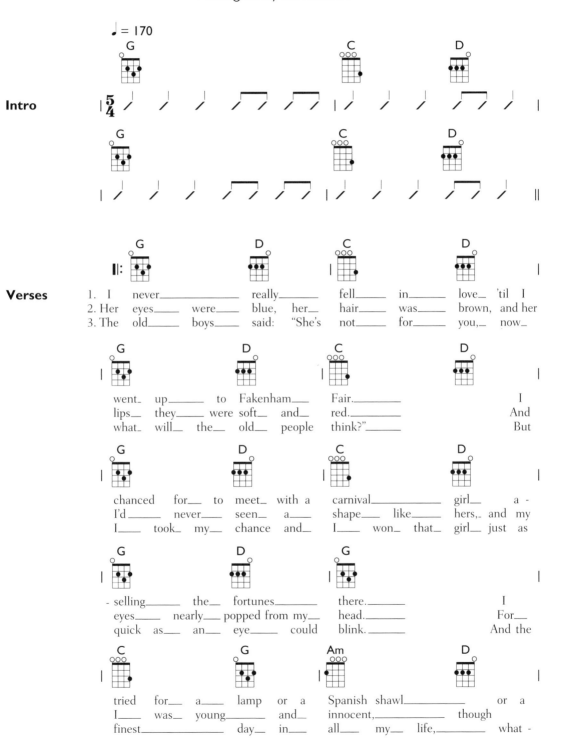

Intro

Verses

1. I never_____ really_____ fell_____ in_____ love_ 'til I
2. Her eyes_____ were_____ blue, her_ hair_____ was_____ brown, and her
3. The old_____ boys_____ said: "She's not_____ for_____ you,_ now_

went_ up_____ to Fakenham___ Fair._____   I
lips_ they_____ were soft_ and_ red._____   And
what_ will_ the_ old_ people think?"_____   But

chanced for__ to meet_ with a carnival_____ girl__ a -
I'd _____ never____ seen_ a____ shape____ like_____ hers,_ and my
I___ took_ my_ chance and_ I___ won_ that_ girl_ just as

- selling_____ the_ fortunes_____ there._____   I
eyes____ nearly___ popped from my__ head._____   For__
quick as__ an__ eye_____ could blink. _____   And the

tried for__ a____ lamp or a Spanish shawl_____ or a
I___ was_ young_____ and_ innocent,_____ though
finest_____ day_ in___ all___ my_ life,_____ what -

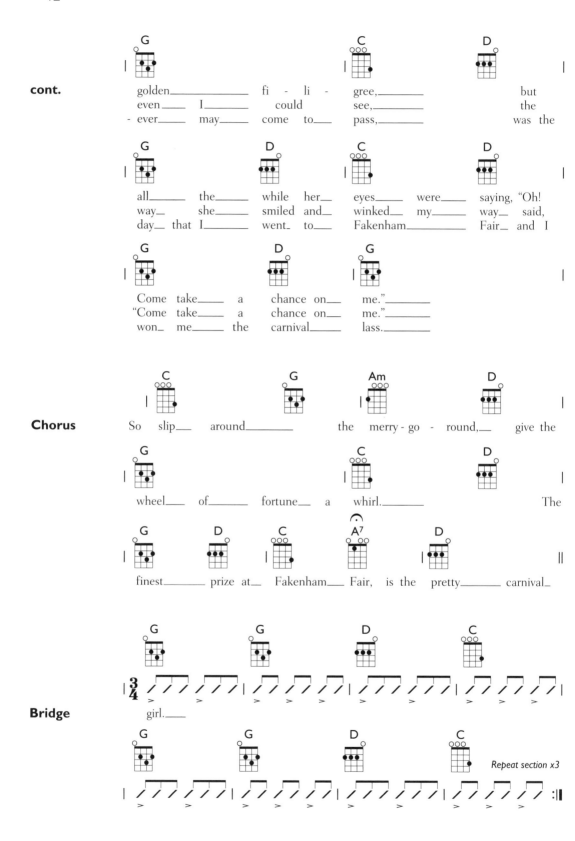

cont.

| G | C | D |

golden———— fi - li - gree,———— but
even—— I———— could see,———— the
- ever—— may—— come to— pass,———— was the

| G | D | C | D |

all—— the—— while her— eyes—— were—— saying, "Oh!
way— she—— smiled and— winked— my—— way— said,
day— that I———— went— to— Fakenham———— Fair— and I

| G | D | G |

Come take—— a chance on— me."————
"Come take—— a chance on— me."————
won— me—— the carnival—— lass.————

Chorus

| C | G | Am | D |

So slip— around———— the merry - go - round,— give the

| G | C | D |

wheel— of—— fortune— a whirl.———— The

| G | D | C | A7 | D |

finest———— prize at— Fakenham— Fair, is the pretty———— carnival_

Bridge

| G | G | D | C |

3/4

girl.——

| G | G | D | C |

Repeat section x3

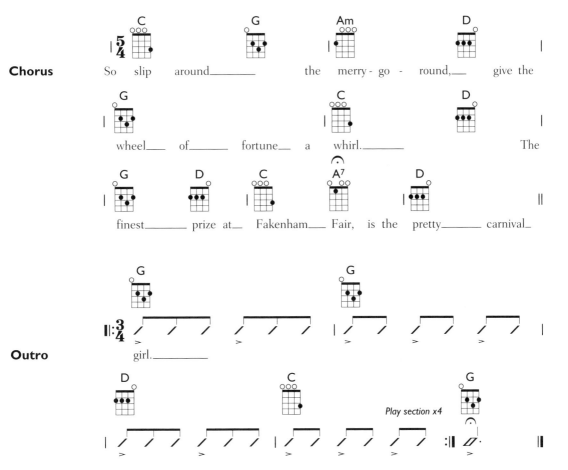

Chorus

So slip around_____ the merry - go - round,_ give the

wheel_ of_____ fortune_ a whirl._____ The

finest_____ prize at_ Fakenham_ Fair, is the pretty_____ carnival_

Outro

girl._____

Play section x4

Foggy Dew

Words by P. O'Neill
Music Traditional
Arranged by Paddy Moloney

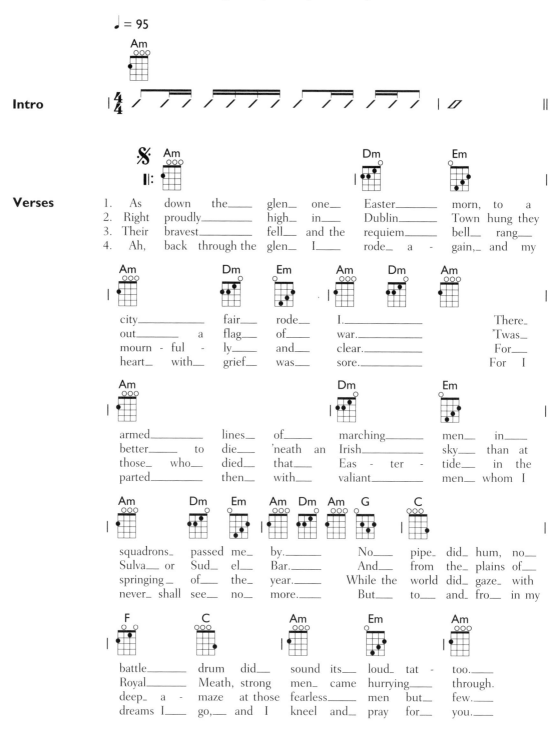

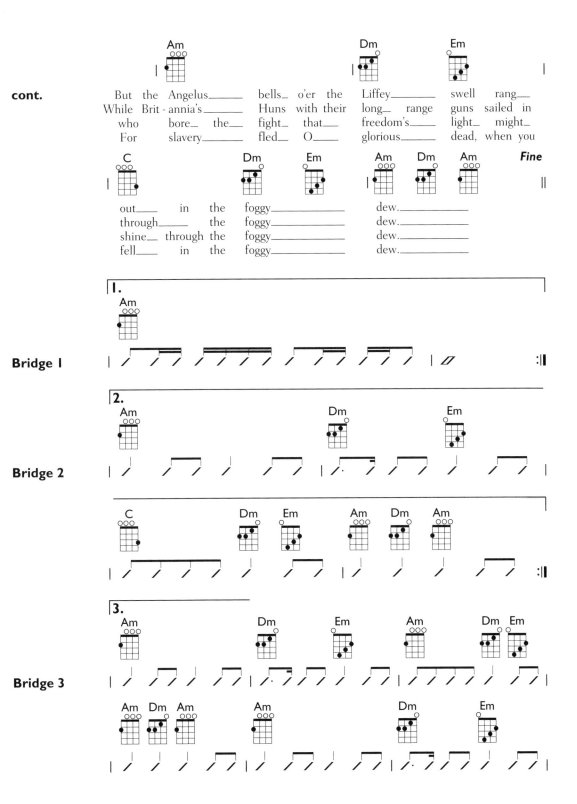

cont.

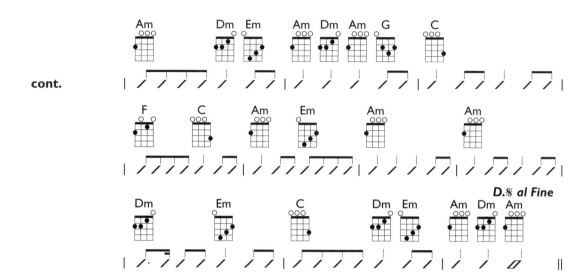

Green Grow The Rushes, O

Words and Music Traditional

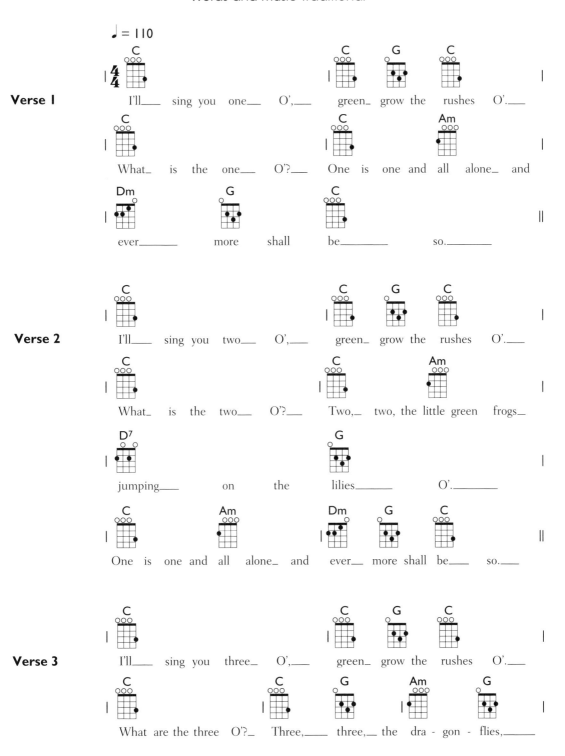

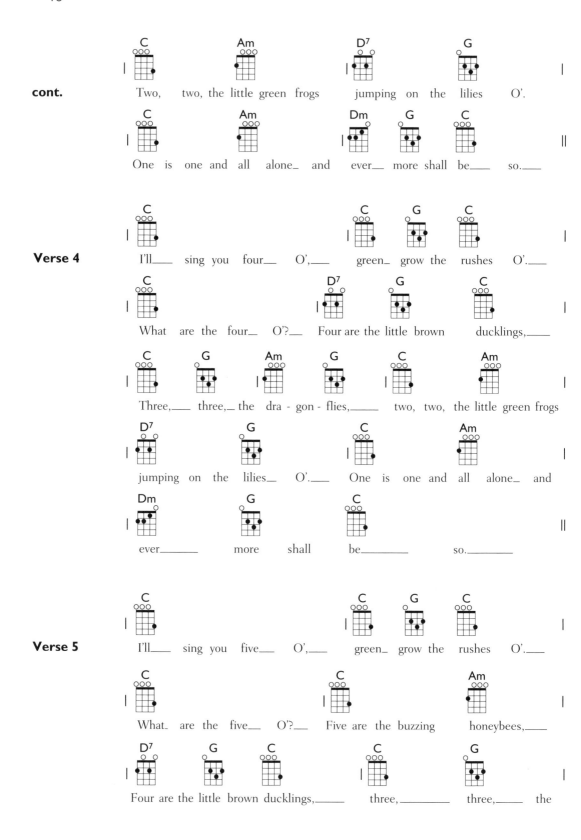

cont.

C — Am — D⁷ — G
| Two, two, the little green frogs | jumping on the lilies O'.

C — Am — Dm G C
| One is one and all alone‿ and | ever‿ more shall be‿ so.‿ ‖

Verse 4

C — C G C
| I'll‿ sing you four‿ O',‿ | green‿ grow the rushes O'.‿ |

C — D⁷ G C
| What are the four‿ O'?‿ Four are the little brown ducklings,‿ |

C G Am G C Am
| Three,‿ three,‿ the dra-gon-flies,‿ two, two, the little green frogs |

D⁷ G C Am
| jumping on the lilies‿ O'.‿ One is one and all alone‿ and |

Dm G C
| ever‿ more shall be‿ so.‿ ‖

Verse 5

C — C G C
| I'll‿ sing you five‿ O',‿ | green‿ grow the rushes O'.‿ |

C — C Am
| What‿ are the five‿ O'?‿ Five are the buzzing honeybees,‿ |

D⁷ G C C G
| Four are the little brown ducklings,‿ three,‿ three,‿ the |

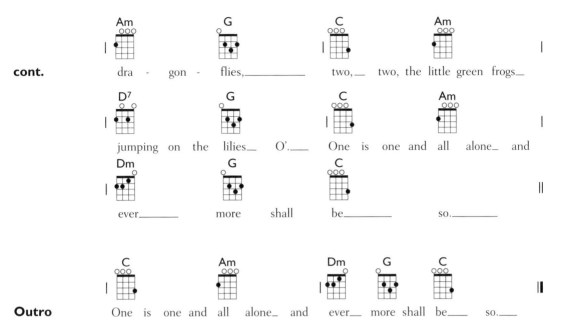

cont.

Am	G	C	Am
dra - gon - flies,_____	two,__ two, the little green frogs__		

D⁷	G	C	Am
jumping on the lilies__ O'.___	One is one and all alone__ and		

Dm	G	C
ever_____ more shall be_____ so._____		

Outro

C	Am	Dm G C
One is one and all alone__ and ever__ more shall be___ so.___		

The Galway Races

Words and Music by Traditional, Ronald Drew,
Barney MacKenna, John Sheahan, Luke Kelly and Ciaran Bourke

♩ = 150

G

‖: 4/4

Verses

1. As I rode out through Galway___ Town
2. There were passengers___ from Limerick___
3. There were multitudes___ from Aran___
4. And it's there you'll see confectioners___
5. And it's there you'll see the gamblers,___
6. And it's there you'll see the pipers___
7. And it's there you'll see the jockeys___
8. There was half a million___ people___

G

to seek for recreation,___
and passengers___ from Nenagh.
and mem - bers from New Quay shore.___
with sugarsticks___ and dainties.
the thimbles___ and the garters.
and the fiddlers___ competing.___
and they mounted___ on so stately.___
there from all denominations.___

Em

on the seventeenth___ of August,___
Passengers___ from Dublin___
The boys from Connemara___
The lozenges___ and oranges,___
And the sporting___ wheel of fortune___
The nimble___ footed___ dancers,___
The pink, the blue, the orange and green,
The Catholic,___ the Protestant,___

D   G

me mind being e - le - va - ted.
and sports - men from Tipperary.___
and the Clare unmarried___ maidens.
the lemonade___ and raisins.___
with the four and twenty___ quarters.___
and they trippin'___ on the daisies.___
the emblem___ of our nation.___
the Jew and Pres - by - terian.___

cont.

G   **D**

There were multitudes_____ as - sem - bled
There were passengers_____ from Kerry____
People____ from Cork city____
Gingerbread_____ and spices____
There was others____ without__ scruple__
There was others____ shoutin' ci - gars and lights
When the bell was rung for starting,__
Yet there was no a - ni - mo - si - ty,

Em   **G**

with their tickets____ at the station.____
and all quarters____ of the nation.____
who were loyal,____ true and faithful.____
to ac - com - mo - date the ladies.____
pelting_____ wattles at poor old Maggy.____
and bills for all the races.____
all the horses____ seemed im - pa - tient.
no matter____ what per - sua - sion.

G

And me eyes began____ to dazzle____
And our member__ Mr_____ Hardy____
They brought home the Fenian__ prisoners_____
And a big crubeen__ for thruppence
And her daddy____ well contented_____
With the colours____ of the jockey____
I thought they never____ stood on ground,
But failte____ hospitality_____

Em

and they're going to see the races._
for to join the Galway____ blazers.
from dying in foreign____ nations.
to be suckin'__ while you're able._
to be gawking_ at his daughter.
and the price and horses____ ages._
their speed was so amazing._____
in - du - cing fresh acquaintance._____

Em **D** **Em**   **Em** :‖

Chorus With me whack, fol de do,_ fol the diddlely idle_ day._____

Greensleeves

Words and Music Traditional

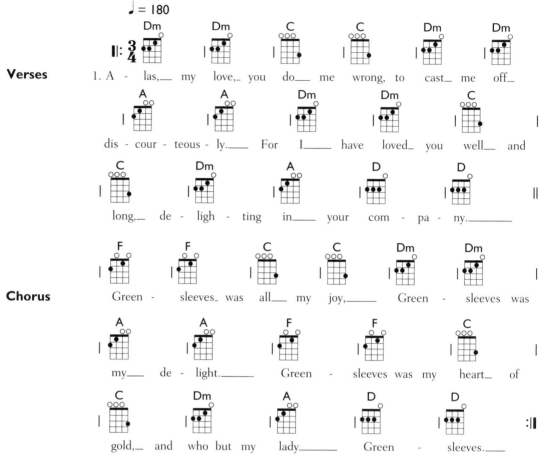

♩ = 180

Verses

1. A - las,__ my love,_ you do__ me wrong, to cast_ me off_

dis - cour - teous - ly.__ For I__ have loved_ you well__ and

long,_ de - ligh - ting in__ your com - pa - ny._____

Chorus

Green - sleeves_ was all__ my joy,_____ Green - sleeves was

my__ de - light._____ Green - sleeves was my heart_ of

gold,_ and who but my lady_____ Green - sleeves.__

Verse 2:
Thy smock of silk, both fair and white,
With gold embroidered gorgeously;
Thy petticoat of sendal right,
And these I bought thee gladly.

Verse 3:
I bought thee kerchiefs for thy head,
That were wrought fine and gallantly;
I kept thee at both board and bed,
Which cost my purse well-favoredly.

Verse 4:
I bought thee petticoats of the best,
The cloth so fine as it might be;
I gave thee jewels for thy chest,
And all this cost I spent on thee.

Verse 5:
I have been ready at your hand,
To grant whatever you would crave,
I have both wagered life and land,
Your love and good-will for to have.

Verse 6:
Your gown was of the grassy green
Your sleeves of satin were hanging by,
Which made you be a harvest queen
Yet you would not love me.

Verse 7:
My men were clothed all in green,
And they did ever wait on thee;
All this was gallant to be seen,
And yet thou wouldst not love me.

Verse 8:
They set thee up, they took thee down,
They served thee with humility;
Thy foot might not once touch the ground,
And yet thou wouldst not love me.

Verse 9:
Thou couldst desire no earthly thing,
But still thou hadst it readily.
Thy music still to play and sing;
And yet thou wouldst not love me.

Verse 10:
If you intend thus to disdain,
It does the more enrapture me,
And even so, I still remain
A lover in captivity.

Verse 11:
Your vows you've broken, like my heart,
Oh, why did you so enrapture me?
Now I remain in a world apart
But my heart remains in captivity.

Verse 12:
Well, I will pray to God on high,
That thou my constancy mayst see,
And that yet once before I die,
Thou wilt vouchsafe to love me.

Verse 13:
Ah, Greensleeves, now farewell, adieu
To God I pray to prosper thee,
For I am still thy lover true,
Come once again and love me.

Here We Come A-Wassailing

Words and Music Traditional

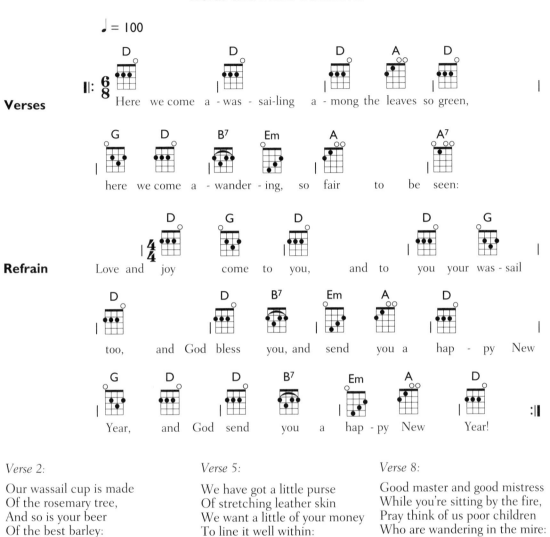

Verses

Here we come a - was - sai - ling a - mong the leaves so green,

here we come a - wander - ing, so fair to be seen:

Refrain

Love and joy come to you, and to you your was - sail

too, and God bless you, and send you a hap - py New

Year, and God send you a hap - py New Year!

Verse 2:

Our wassail cup is made
Of the rosemary tree,
And so is your beer
Of the best barley:

Verse 3:

We are not daily beggars
That beg from door to door,
But we are neighbours' children
Whom you have seen before:

Verse 4:

Call up the butler of this house,
Put on his golden ring;
Let him bring us up a glass of beer
And better we shall sing:

Verse 5:

We have got a little purse
Of stretching leather skin
We want a little of your money
To line it well within:

Verse 6:

Bring us out a table,
And spread it with a cloth;
Bring us out a mouldy cheese,
And some of your Christmas loaf:

Verse 7:

God bless the master of this house,
Likewise the mistress too;
And all the little children
That round the table go:

Verse 8:

Good master and good mistress
While you're sitting by the fire,
Pray think of us poor children
Who are wandering in the mire:

The House Of The Rising Sun

Words and Music Traditional

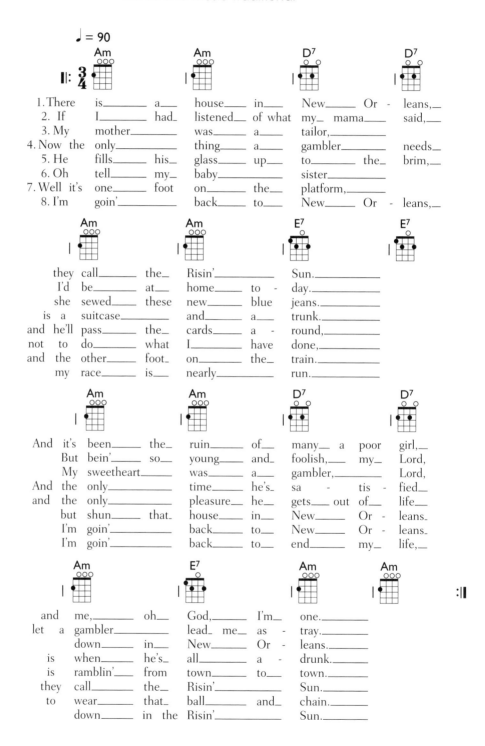

♩ = 90

Verses

1. There is_____ a___ house____ in___ New_____ Or - leans,___
2. If I_____ had_ listened___ of what my_ mama_____ said,___
3. My mother_____ was_____ a___ tailor,_____
4. Now the only_____ thing_____ a___ gambler_____ needs__
5. He fills_____ his__ glass_____ up__ to_____ the_ brim,__
6. Oh tell_____ my__ baby_____ sister_____
7. Well it's one_____ foot on_____ the_ platform,_____
8. I'm goin'_____ back_____ to__ New_____ Or - leans,___

they call_____ the_ Risin'_____ Sun._____
I'd be_____ at__ home_____ to - day._____
she sewed_____ these new_____ blue jeans._____
is a suitcase_____ and_____ a___ trunk._____
and he'll pass_____ the_ cards_____ a - round,_____
not to do_____ what I_____ have done,_____
and the other_____ foot_ on_____ the_ train._____
my race_____ is___ nearly_____ run._____

And it's been_____ the_ ruin_____ of__ many__ a poor girl,__
But bein'_____ so__ young_____ and_ foolish,___ my_ Lord,
My sweetheart_____ was_____ a___ gambler,_____ Lord,
And the only_____ time_____ he's_ sa - tis - fied__
and the only_____ pleasure__ he__ gets__ out of__ life__
but shun_____ that_ house_____ in__ New_____ Or - leans_
I'm goin'_____ back_____ to__ New_____ Or - leans_
I'm goin'_____ back_____ to__ end_____ my_ life,__

and me,_____ oh__ God,_____ I'm_ one._____
let a gambler_____ lead_ me_ as - tray._____
down_____ in__ New_____ Or - leans._____
is when_____ he's_ all_____ a - drunk._____
is ramblin'___ from town_____ to__ town._____
they call_____ the_ Risin'_____ Sun._____
to wear_____ that_ ball_____ and_ chain._____
down_____ in the Risin'_____ Sun._____

The Lincolnshire Poacher

Words and Music Traditional

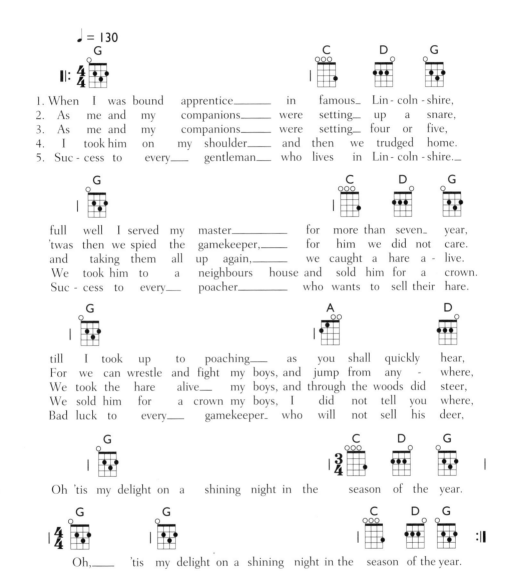

Verses

1. When I was bound apprentice_____ in famous_ Lin - coln - shire,
2. As me and my companions_____ were setting_ up a snare,
3. As me and my companions_____ were setting_ four or five,
4. I took him on my shoulder____ and then we trudged home.
5. Suc - cess to every__ gentleman__ who lives in Lin - coln - shire._

full well I served my master_____ for more than seven_ year,
'twas then we spied the gamekeeper,_____ for him we did not care.
and taking them all up again,_____ we caught a hare a - live.
We took him to a neighbours house and sold him for a crown.
Suc - cess to every__ poacher_____ who wants to sell their hare.

till I took up to poaching___ as you shall quickly hear,
For we can wrestle and fight my boys, and jump from any - where,
We took the hare alive__ my boys, and through the woods did steer,
We sold him for a crown my boys, I did not tell you where,
Bad luck to every__ gamekeeper_ who will not sell his deer,

Refrain

Oh 'tis my delight on a shining night in the season of the year.

Oh,____ 'tis my delight on a shining night in the season of the year.

John Barleycorn

Words and Music Traditional

♩ = 100

Am | **C**

Verses

1. There were___ three men___ come_ out of___ the West, their
2. They let____ him_ lie___ for a long, long___ time, till the
3. They hired_____ men_ with the scythes so sharp to
4. So they dragged him a - round and a - round the___ field till they
5. There's little___ Sir___ John___ in a nut_ brown bowl, and

G | **Am**

fortunes_____ for_____ to_____ try._____ And
rains_____ from heaven_ did____ fall._____ And
cut him___ off at_____ the____ knee.____ They
came_____ un - to_____ a_____ barn._____ And
brandy_____ in_____ a_____ glass._____ But

Am | **C**

these_ three_ men_ made a solemn_____ vow,_____ John
little_ Sir___ John_ sprang_ up___ his___ head_____ and
rolled_ him and tied__ him a - round_ the___ waist,_____
here_ they_ made_ a solemn_____ mow_____ of
little_ Sir___ John_ with his nut__ brown bowl_ he'll slay the

G | **Am**

Barleycorn_____ would_ die._____ They've
he____ amazed_____ them__ all._____ They
treated him most bar - ba - rous - ly._____ They
poor__ John___ Bar - ley - corn.____ They
strongest_____ man___ at_____ last.____ For the

C | **G**

ploughed, they've_ sown,_ they've harrowed__ him in,___ thrown
let___ him___ stand_ for a long, long time, and he
hired_____ men_ with the sharp_ edged_ forks___ to
hired_____ men_ with the crabtree_____ sticks____ to
huntsman_____ he___ can't_ hunt_ the___ fox,_____ nor

cont.

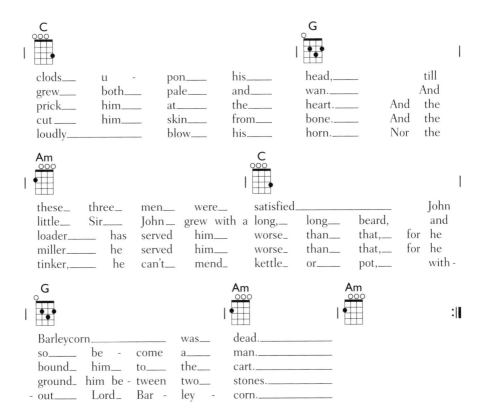

C				G	
clods—	u -	pon—	his—	head,—	till
grew—	both—	pale—	and—	wan.—	And
prick—	him—	at—	the—	heart.—	And the
cut—	him—	skin—	from—	bone.—	And the
loudly—		blow—	his—	horn.—	Nor the

Am				C		John
these—	three—	men—	were—	satisfied—		John
little—	Sir—	John—	grew with a	long,—	long— beard,	and
loader—	has	served	him—	worse—	than— that,—	for he
miller—	he	served	him—	worse—	than— that,—	for he
tinker,—	he	can't—	mend—	kettle—	or— pot,—	with -

G				Am	Am
Barleycorn—			was—	dead.—	
so—	be -	come	a—	man.—	
bound—	him—	to—	the—	cart.—	
ground—	him be -	tween	two—	stones.—	
- out—	Lord—	Bar -	ley -	corn.—	

:‖

John Henry

Words and Music Traditional

♩ = 130

D

‖: 4/4

D

Verses

1. John___ Henry,_____ when he was a baby,_____
2. Well there's some said_ he's born down in Texas,_____
3. Well the captain_____ said to John_ Henry,_____
4. John___ Henry_____ said to__ the captain,_____
5. John___ Henry_____ said to__ his shaker,_____
6. Well the shaker_____ said to John_ Henry,_____ "Well a
7. John___ Henry_____ had a little_ woman,_____ her
8. They__ took_ John_ Henry to the graveyard,___

D   **A⁷**

sitting _ on his mammy's _____ knee,_____
some said____ he's born up__ in Maine._____
"I'm gonna bring my steam_ drill__ round._____ Gonna
"Bring__ your__ steam_ drill a - round._____ You can
"Shaker,_____ you had better pray._____
man___ ain't__ nothing but a man._____ I'm a
name__ was__ Polly - Anne._____ John
laid____ him__ down_ in the sand._____

D   **D**

picked up_____ a hammer in his little_ right hand, saying___
I_____ just_ said he was a Louisianna man,___
bring___ my_ steam_ drill___ out on_ this job,_ I'm gonna
bring___ your_ steam_ drill___ out on_ the job,_ I'm gonna
If_____ you_ miss___ your___ six feet_ of steel,
throw in a hundred pound_ from my hips_ on_ down,___
Henry_____ took_ sick___ and was laid up_ in bed,___ while
Every_____ locomotive_____ comin' a rollin'_____ by_ hollered,

D   **D**

"That'll be__ the death_ of____ me,_ me,_ me,_____
leader_ of a steel_ driving chain_____ gang,_____
pop__ that_____ steel_ on__ down, down, down._____
beat__ your_____ steam_ drill__ down, down, down,_____
to - mor - row be your burying_____ day,_ day,_ day._____
doing all__ that any__ man__ can,_ can,_ can._____
Polly__ handled____ steel_ like a man,_ man,_ man._____
"There lies_ a steel_ driving man,_ man,_ man._____

cont.

D		A⁷		D	

that'll be___ the death_ of___ me.___
leader_ of a steel__ driving gang.___
Pop___ that_____ steel__ on___ down.___ I'm gonna
beat___ your_____ steam_ drill__ down.___ Gonna
To - mor - row be your burying_____ day.___ To -
Doing all___ that any___ man__ can.___
Polly__ handled___ steel__ like a man.___
There lies___ a steel__ driving man.___

D		D

That'll be___ the death of_____ me,__ me,__ me,_____
Leader of a steel_ driving___ chain_____ gang,_____
pop___ that_____ steel_ on_____ down, down, down._____
beat___ your_____ steam drill_____ down, down, down,_____
- mor - row be your burying_____ day,__ day,__ day._____ To -
Doing all___ that any__ man_____ can,__ can,__ can._____
Polly__ handled___ steel_ like a man,__ man,__ man,_____
There lies__ a steel_ driving___ man,__ man,__ man._____

D		A⁷		D		D	

that'll be___ the death of_____ me."__
leader_ of a steel_ driving___ gang._
Pop___ that_____ steel_ on_____ down."
beat___ your_____ steam drill_____ down."
-mor - row be your burying_____ day."__
Doing all___ that any_ man_____ can."__
Polly__ handled___ steel_ like a man._
There lies___ a steel_ driving___ man."__

Morning Has Broken

Words and Music Traditional

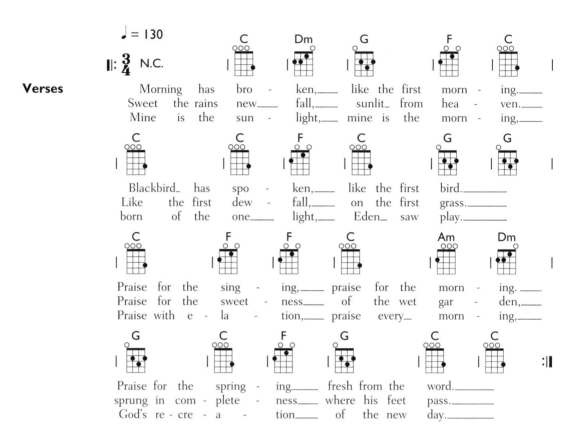

Verses

Morning has bro - ken,___ like the first morn - ing.___
Sweet the rains new___ fall,___ sunlit___ from hea - ven.___
Mine is the sun - light,___ mine is the morn - ing,___

Blackbird___ has spo - ken,___ like the first bird._____
Like the first dew - fall,___ on the first grass._____
born of the one___ light,___ Eden___ saw play._____

Praise for the sing - ing,___ praise for the morn - ing. ___
Praise for the sweet - ness___ of the wet gar - den,___
Praise with e - la - tion,___ praise every___ morn - ing,___

Praise for the spring - ing___ fresh from the word._____
sprung in com - plete - ness___ where his feet pass._____
God's re - cre - a - tion___ of the new day._____

Matty Groves

Words and Music Traditional
Arranged by Simon Nicol, David Mattacks,
Sandy Denny, Ashley Hutchings and Richard Thompson

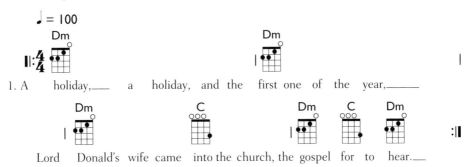

Verse 2:
And when the meeting it was done
She cast her eyes about
And there she saw little Matty Groves
Walking in the crowd.

Verse 3:
"Come home with me, little Matty Groves,
Come home with me tonight.
Come home with me, little Matty Groves
And sleep with me 'til light."

Verse 4:
"Oh I can't come home, I won't come home
And sleep with you tonight!
By the rings on your fingers I can tell
You are Lord Donald's wife."

Verse 5:
"What if I am Lord Donald's wife,
Lord Donald's not at home.
He is out in the far cornfields,
Bringing the yearlings home."

Instrumental verse

Verse 6:
And a servant who was standing by
And hearing what was said
He swore Lord Donald he would know
Before the sun would set.

Verse 7:
And in his hurry to carry the news
He bent his breast and ran
And when he came to the broad mill stream
He took off his shoes and swam.

Instrumental verse

Verse 8:
Little Matty Groves he lay down
And took a little sleep
When he awoke, Lord Donald
Was standing at his feet

Verse 9:
Saying "How do you like my feather bed?
And how do you like my sheets?
How do you like my lady
Who lies in your arms asleep?"

Verse 10:
"Oh well I like your feather bed
And well I like your sheets
But better I like your lady wife
Who lies in my arms asleep."

Verse 11:
"Well, get up! Get up!" Lord Donald cried
"Get up as quick as you can!
It'll never be said in fair England
I slew a naked man."

Verse 12:
"Oh I can't get up, I won't get up
I can't get up for my life!
For you have two long beaten swords
And I not a pocket knife."

Verse 13:
"Well it's true I have two beaten swords
And they cost me deep in the purse.
But you will have the better of them
And I will have the worse.

Verse 14:
And you will strike the very first blow
And strike it like a man!
I will strike the very next blow
And I'll kill you if I can."

Instrumental verse

Verse 15:
So Matty struck the very first blow
And he hurt Lord Donald sore.
Lord Donald struck the very next blow
And Matty struck no more.

Verse 16:
And then Lord Donald he took his wife
And he sat her upon his knee
Saying, "Who do you like the best of us,
Matty Groves or me?"

Verse 17:
And then up spoke his own dear wife,
Never heard to speak so free
"I'd rather a kiss from dead Matty's lips
Than you or your finery."

Instrumental verse

Verse 18:
Lord Donald he jumped up
And loudly he did bawl
He struck his wife right through the heart
And pinned her against the wall.

Verse 19:
"A grave, a grave!" Lord Donald cried
"To put these lovers in!
But bury my lady at the top
For she was of noble kin."

Final instrumental verse

My Bonnie Lies Over The Ocean

Words and Music Traditional

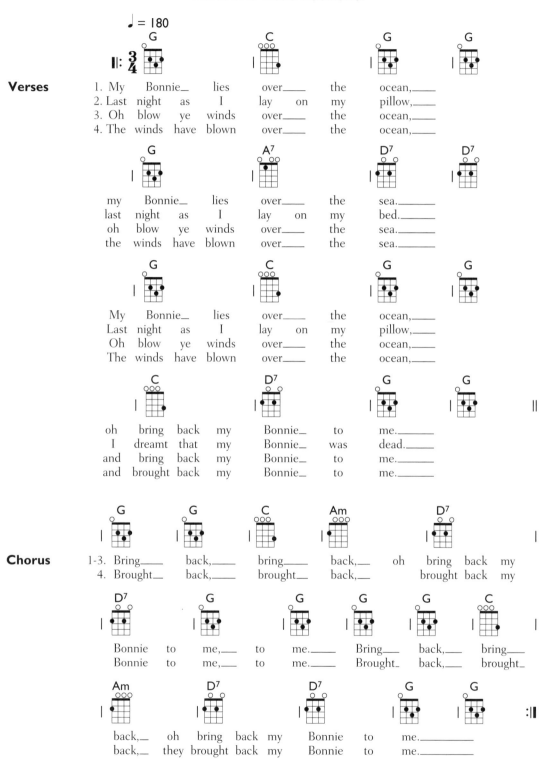

Verses

1. My Bonnie lies over the ocean,
2. Last night as I lay on my pillow,
3. Oh blow ye winds over the ocean,
4. The winds have blown over the ocean,

my Bonnie lies over the sea.
last night as I lay on my bed.
oh blow ye winds over the sea.
the winds have blown over the sea.

My Bonnie lies over the ocean,
Last night as I lay on my pillow,
Oh blow ye winds over the ocean,
The winds have blown over the ocean,

oh bring back my Bonnie to me.
I dreamt that my Bonnie was dead.
and bring back my Bonnie to me.
and brought back my Bonnie to me.

Chorus

1-3. Bring back, bring back, oh bring back my
4. Brought back, brought back, oh brought back my

Bonnie to me, to me. Bring back, bring
Bonnie to me, to me. Brought back, brought

back, oh bring back my Bonnie to me.
back, they brought back my Bonnie to me.

My Love Is Like A Red, Red Rose

Scottish Traditional

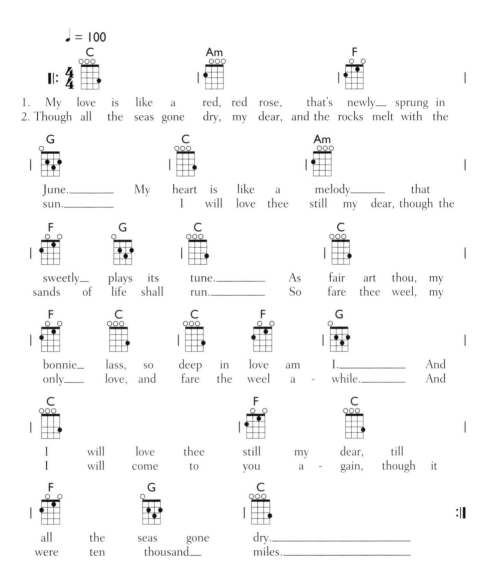

Verses

1. My love is like a red, red rose, that's newly‿ sprung in
2. Though all the seas gone dry, my dear, and the rocks melt with the

June._____ My heart is like a melody_____ that
sun._____ I will love thee still my dear, though the

sweetly‿ plays its tune._____ As fair art thou, my
sands of life shall run._____ So fare thee weel, my

bonnie‿ lass, so deep in love am I._____ And
only‿ love, and fare the weel a - while._____ And

I will love thee still my dear, till
I will come to you a - gain, though it

all the seas gone dry._____
were ten thousand‿ miles._____

Over The Hills And Far Away

Words and Music Traditional

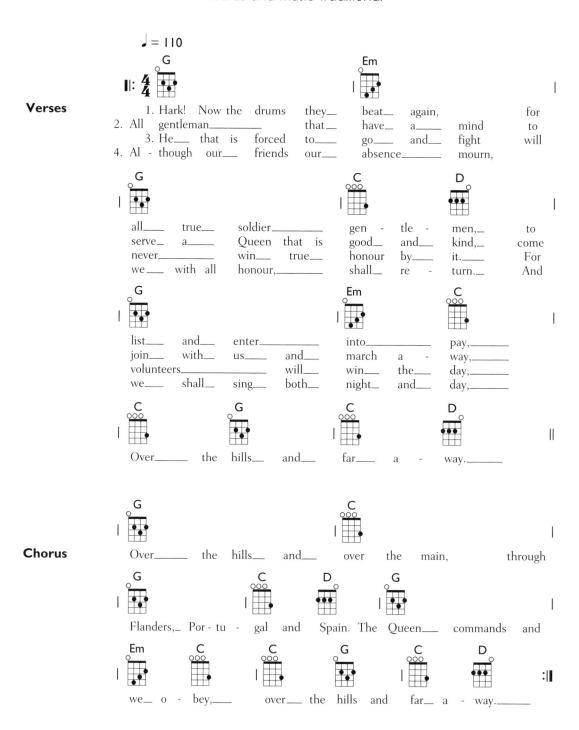

Verses

♩ = 110

G	Em
Hark! Now the drums they_ beat_ again, for	
2. All gentleman_ that_ have_ a_ mind to	
3. He_ that is forced to_ go_ and_ fight will	
4. Al - though our_ friends our_ absence_ mourn,	

G / C / D

all_ true_ soldier_ gen - tle - men,_ to
serve_ a_ Queen that is good_ and_ kind,_ come
never_ win_ true_ honour by_ it._ For
we_ with all honour,_ shall_ re - turn._ And

G / Em / C

list_ and_ enter_ into_ pay,_
join_ with_ us_ and_ march a - way,_
volunteers_ will_ win_ the_ day,_
we_ shall_ sing_ both_ night_ and_ day,_

C / G / C / D

Over_ the hills_ and_ far_ a - way._

Chorus

G / C

Over_ the hills_ and_ over the main, through

G / C / D / G

Flanders,_ Por - tu - gal and Spain. The Queen_ commands and

Em / C / C / G / C / D

we_ o - bey,_ over_ the hills and far_ a - way._

The Parting Glass

Words and Music Traditional

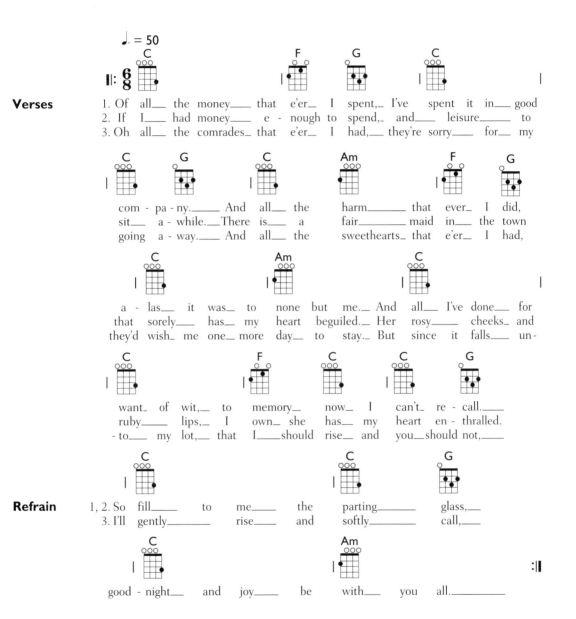

Verses

1. Of all__ the money____ that e'er__ I spent,__ I've spent it in__ good
2. If I___ had money____ e - nough to spend,__ and___ leisure_____ to
3. Oh all__ the comrades_ that e'er__ I had,__ they're sorry____ for__ my

com - pa - ny.____ And all__ the harm_____ that ever_ I did,
sit__ a - while.__There is___ a fair_____ maid in__ the town
going a - way.___ And all__ the sweethearts_ that e'er__ I had,

a - las__ it was__ to none but me.__ And all__ I've done__ for
that sorely____ has__ my heart beguiled.__ Her rosy_____ cheeks_ and
they'd wish_ me one__ more day__ to stay.__ But since it falls___ un-

want_ of wit,__ to memory__ now_ I can't_ re - call.____
ruby_____ lips,__ I own_ she has__ my heart en - thralled.
- to__ my lot,__ that I___should rise_ and you__should not,____

Refrain

1, 2. So fill_____ to me____ the parting_____ glass,__
3. I'll gently_____ rise____ and softly_____ call,__

good - night__ and joy_____ be with__ you all._____

Raggle Taggle Gypsy

Words and Music Traditional

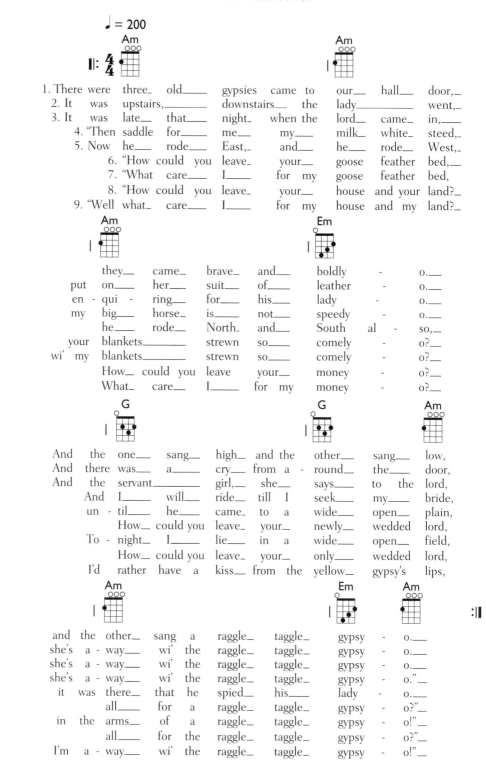

Verses

♩ = 200

Am

1. There were three old gypsies came to our hall door,
2. It was upstairs, downstairs the lady went,
3. It was late that night when the lord came in,
4. "Then saddle for me my milk white steed,
5. Now he rode East, and he rode West,
6. "How could you leave your goose feather bed,
7. "What care I for my goose feather bed,
8. "How could you leave your house and your land?
9. "Well what care I for my house and my land?

Am   Em

         they came brave and boldly - o.
put on her suit of leather - o.
en - qui - ring for his lady - o.
my big horse is not speedy - o.
he rode North and South al - so,
your blankets strewn so comely - o?
wi' my blankets strewn so comely - o?
How could you leave your money - o?
What care I for my money - o?

G   G   Am

And the one sang high and the other sang low,
And there was a cry from a - round the door,
And the servant girl, she says to the lord,
And I will ride till I seek my bride,
un - til he came to a wide open plain,
How could you leave your newly wedded lord,
To - night I lie in a wide open field,
How could you leave your only wedded lord,
I'd rather have a kiss from the yellow gypsy's lips,

Am   Em   Am

and the other sang a raggle taggle gypsy - o.
she's a - way wi' the raggle taggle gypsy - o.
she's a - way wi' the raggle taggle gypsy - o.
she's a - way wi' the raggle taggle gypsy - o."
it was there that he spied his lady - o.
all for a raggle taggle gypsy - o?
in the arms of a raggle taggle gypsy - o!"
all for the raggle taggle gypsy - o?"
I'm a - way wi' the raggle taggle gypsy - o!"

Faber Music's Ukulele Song Finder

Are you looking for a particular song arranged specifically for ukulele? This useful alphabetical song finder will help you identify which book contains the song you are looking for. Faber Music publishes a wealth of ukulele books suitable for players from absolute beginner to intermediate level.

The Ukulele Playlist: Yellow Book
ISBN 0-571-53328-0

The Ukulele Rock Playlist: Black Book
ISBN 0-571-53565-8

The Ukulele Playlist: Orange Book
ISBN 0-571-53616-6

The Ukulele Playlist: Christmas
ISBN 0-571-53358-2

The Ukulele Playlist: Blue Book
ISBN 0-571-53327-2

The Ukulele Playlist: White Book
ISBN 0-571-53391-4

The Ukulele Playlist: Red Book
ISBN 0-571-533390-6

The Ukulele Jazz Playlist: Purple Book
ISBN 0-571-53566-6

The Ukulele Playlist: Green Book
ISBN 0-571-53645-X

The Ukulele Playlist: Shows
ISBN 0-571-53773-1

The Ukulele Playlist: Kids' Songs
ISBN 0-571-53715-4

The Really Easy Uke Book
ISBN 0-571-53374-4

Ukulele Basics
ISBN 0-571-53588-7

Easy Uke Library: Over The Rainbow
ISBN 0-571-53608-5

Easy Uke Library: Bare Necessities
ISBN 0-571-53606-9

Easy Uke Library: Memory
ISBN 0-571-53607-7

FABER ff MUSIC

Ukulele Song Finder

1,2,3,4 *The Ukulele Playlist: Green Book*
Agadou Dou Dou *The Ukulele Playlist: Kids' Songs Book*
Ain't Misbehavin' *The Ukulele Playlist: Purple Book*
All Along The Watchtower *The Ukulele Playlist: White Book & The Really Easy Uke Book*
All Day And All Of The Night *The Ukulele Playlist: Black Book*
Aloha Oe *The Ukulele Playlist: Green Book*
Always Look On The Bright Side Of Life *The Ukulele Playlist: Blue Book*
Amazing Grace *The Really Easy Uke Book*
American Idiot *The Ukulele Playlist: Red Book*
And All That Jazz *The Ukulele Playlist: Shows Book*
Angels *The Ukulele Playlist: White Book*
Angels From The Realms Of Glory *The Ukulele Playlist: Christmas Book*
Animals Went In Two By Two, The *The Ukulele Playlist: Kids' Songs Book*
Any Dream Will Do *The Ukulele Playlist: Shows Book*
Anything Goes *The Ukulele Playlist: Green Book*
Auld Lang Syne *The Ukulele Playlist: Christmas Book*
Autumn Leaves *The Ukulele Playlist: Purple Book*
Away In A Manger *The Ukulele Playlist: Christmas Book*
Babooshka *The Ukulele Playlist: Yellow Book*
Back For Good *The Ukulele Playlist: Blue Book*
Back In Black *The Ukulele Playlist: Red Book*
Bad Moon Rising *The Ukulele Playlist: Yellow Book*
Banana Boat Song, The *The Ukulele Playlist: Green Book & Ukulele Basics*
Bare Necessities, The *The Ukulele Playlist: Kids' Songs Book*
Basket Case *The Ukulele Playlist: Black Book*
Beat It *The Ukulele Playlist: Yellow Book*
Beep Beep Song *The Ukulele Playlist: Yellow Book*
Bewitched *The Ukulele Playlist: Purple Book*
Bibbidi Bobbidi Boo *The Ukulele Playlist: Kids' Songs Book*
Bill Bailey, Won't You Please Come Home *The Ukulele Playlist: Green Book*
Birdie Song *The Ukulele Playlist: Kids' Songs Book*
Bittersweet Symphony *The Ukulele Playlist: Blue Book*
Blue Christmas *The Ukulele Playlist: Christmas Book*
Blue Moon *The Ukulele Playlist: White Book & Ukulele Basics*
Boar's Head Carol *The Ukulele Playlist: Christmas Book*
Boulevard Of Broken Dreams *The Ukulele Playlist: Yellow Book*
Breakfast At Tiffany's *The Ukulele Playlist: Yellow Book*
Bright Eyes *The Ukulele Playlist: White Book*
Buckingham Palace *The Ukulele Playlist: Kids' Songs Book*
Build Me Up Buttercup *The Ukulele Playlist: Blue Book*
By The Light Of The Silvery Moon *The Ukulele Playlist: Green Book*
Cabaret *The Ukulele Playlist: Shows Book*
Call Me *The Ukulele Playlist: Red Book*
Candy *The Ukulele Playlist: Red Book*
Can't Get You Out Of My Head *The Ukulele Playlist: White Book*
Can You Feel The Love Tonight *The Ukulele Playlist: Shows Book*
Christmas Song, The (Chestnuts Roasting On An Open Fire) *The Ukulele Playlist: Christmas Book*
Circle Of Life *The Ukulele Playlist: Kids' Songs Book*
Clementine *Ukulele Basics*
Cockles And Mussels *The Ukulele Playlist: Kids' Songs Book*
Coffee & TV *The Ukulele Playlist: White Book*
Come Away With Me *The Ukulele Playlist: Purple Book*
Come On Eileen *The Ukulele Playlist: Blue Book*
Complicated *The Ukulele Playlist: Orange Book*
Consider Yourself *The Ukulele Playlist: Shows Book*
Cotton Fields (The Cotton Song) *The Ukulele Playlist: Green Book*
Crazy *The Ukulele Playlist: Yellow Book & The Ukulele Playlist: Orange Book*
Crazy Little Thing Called Love *The Ukulele Playlist: Blue Book*
Creep *The Ukulele Playlist: Blue Book*
Cry Me A River *The Ukulele Playlist: Purple Book*
Daisy Bell *Ukulele Basics & The Ukulele Playlist: Kids' Songs Book*
Dancing In The Moonlight *The Ukulele Playlist: Orange Book*
Danny Boy *The Really Easy Uke Book*
Daydream Believer *The Ukulele Playlist: Blue Book*
Deadwood Stage, The *The Ukulele Playlist: Kids' Songs Book*
Deck The Halls *The Ukulele Playlist: Christmas Book*

Delilah *The Really Easy Uke Book*
Ding Dong Merrily On High *The Ukulele Playlist: Christmas Book*
Dingle Dangle Scarecrow *The Ukulele Playlist: Kids' Songs Book*
Dirty Old Town *The Really Easy Uke Book*
Do They Know It's Christmas *The Ukulele Playlist: Christmas Book*
Don't Fence Me In *The Ukulele Playlist: Green Book*
Don't Get Me Wrong *The Ukulele Playlist: Blue Book*
Don't Leave Me This Way *The Ukulele Playlist: Shows Book*
Don't Look Back Into The Sun *The Ukulele Playlist: Black Book*
Don't Rain On My Parade *The Ukulele Playlist: Shows Book*
Don't Stop Believin' *The Ukulele Playlist: Black Book*
Don't Stop Me Now *The Ukulele Playlist: Red Book*
Don't You Want Me *The Ukulele Playlist: White Book*
Down Under *The Ukulele Playlist: White Book*
Dreadlock Holiday *The Ukulele Playlist: Red Book*
Dream A Little Dream Of Me *The Ukulele Playlist: Yellow Book*
Drunken Sailor! *Ukulele Basics*
Early One Morning *The Ukulele Playlist: Green Book & The Really Easy Uke Book*
Easy *The Ukulele Playlist: Red Book*
Edelweiss *The Really Easy Uke Book & The Ukulele Playlist: Shows Book*
Embraceable You *The Ukulele Playlist: Purple Book*
Ever Fallen In Love With Someone You Shouldn't've *The Ukulele Playlist: Red Book*
Everybody Needs Somebody *The Ukulele Playlist: White Book*
Fairy Tale Of New York *The Ukulele Playlist: Christmas Book*
Faith *The Ukulele Playlist: White Book*
Fame *The Ukulele Playlist: Orange Book*
Fascinating Rhythm *The Ukulele Playlist: Purple Book*
Fear, The *The Ukulele Playlist: Red Book*
Feed The Birds *The Ukulele Playlist: Kids' Songs Book*
Fell In Love With A Girl *The Ukulele Playlist: Red Book*
Fisherman's Blues *The Ukulele Playlist: Yellow Book*
Flagpole Sitta *The Ukulele Playlist: Blue Book*
Fluorescent Adolescent *The Ukulele Playlist: Blue Book*
Foggy Day, A *The Ukulele Playlist: Purple Book*
Food, Glorious Food *The Ukulele Playlist: Kids' Songs Book*
Foundations *The Ukulele Playlist: Blue Book*
Frankie *The Ukulele Playlist: Orange Book*
Frère Jacques *Ukulele Basics*
From Both Sides Now *The Ukulele Playlist: Green Book*
Frosty The Snowman *The Ukulele Playlist: Christmas Book*
Get It On *The Ukulele Playlist: Black Book*
Get Me To The Church On Time *The Really Easy Uke Book*
Ghostbusters *The Ukulele Playlist: Kids' Songs Book*
Gigi *The Ukulele Playlist: Shows Book*
Go Your Own Way *The Ukulele Playlist: Blue Book*
Good King Wenceslas *The Ukulele Playlist: Christmas Book*
Grandma Got Run Over By A Reindeer *The Ukulele Playlist: Christmas Book*
Grease *The Ukulele Playlist: Orange Book*
Greased Lightnin' *The Really Easy Uke Book*
Great Balls Of Fire *The Ukulele Playlist: White Book*
Greatest Day *The Ukulele Playlist: White Book*
Green Door, The *The Ukulele Playlist: Green Book*
Green Grow The Rushes, O *The Ukulele Playlist: Kids' Songs Book*
Grenade *The Ukulele Playlist: Orange Book*
Ha Ha This A Way *The Ukulele Playlist: Green Book*
Happy Birthday To You *The Really Easy Uke Book*
Happy Together *The Ukulele Playlist: Blue Book*
Hark! The Herald Angels Sing *The Ukulele Playlist: Christmas Book*
Have Yourself A Merry Little Christmas *The Ukulele Playlist: Christmas Book*
Hello Dolly *The Ukulele Playlist: Shows Book*
Here I Go Again *The Ukulele Playlist: Black Book & The Ukulele Playlist: Shows Book*
Here We Come A-Wassailing *The Ukulele Playlist: Christmas Book*
He's Got The Whole World In His Hands *Ukulele Basics*
Hey There Delilah *The Ukulele Playlist: Red Book*
Higher Ground *The Ukulele Playlist: White Book*
Hippopotamus Song, The *The Really Easy Uke Book & The Ukulele Playlist: Kids' Songs Book*

Hit The Road Jack *The Ukulele Playlist: Blue Book & The Ukulele Playlist: Purple Book*

Hokey Cokey, The *The Ukulele Playlist: Kids' Songs Book*

Holly & The Ivy, The *The Ukulele Playlist: Christmas Book*

Hotel California *The Ukulele Playlist: Blue Book*

Hounds Of Love *The Ukulele Playlist: Black Book*

House Of Fun *The Ukulele Playlist: Blue Book*

House Of The Rising Sun, The *The Ukulele Playlist: Yellow Book & The Really Easy Uke Book*

How Deep Is Your Love *The Ukulele Playlist: Yellow Book*

How Much Is That Doggie In The Window *The Really Easy Uke Book & Ukulele Basics*

Hush *The Ukulele Playlist: Yellow Book*

I Am The Very Model Of A Modern Major General *The Ukulele Playlist: Shows Book*

I Am What I Am *The Ukulele Playlist: Orange Book & The Ukulele Playlist: Shows Book*

I Can See Clearly Now *The Ukulele Playlist: Red Book*

I Do Like To Be Beside The Seaside *The Really Easy Uke Book*

I Don't Feel Like Dancin' *The Ukulele Playlist: Yellow Book*

I Don't Wanna Dance *The Ukulele Playlist: White Book*

I Get A Kick Out Of You *The Ukulele Playlist: Shows Book*

I Got Plenty O' Nuttin' *The Ukulele Playlist: Shows Book*

I Got Rhythm *The Ukulele Playlist: Shows Book*

I Got You Babe *The Ukulele Playlist: Red Book*

I Have A Dream *The Really Easy Uke Book*

I Love Rock N Roll *The Ukulele Playlist: Black Book*

I Only Want To Be With You *The Ukulele Playlist: Green Book*

I Saw Mommy Kissing Santa Claus *The Ukulele Playlist: Christmas Book*

I Wanna Be Like You *The Ukulele Playlist: Blue Book, The Really Easy Uke Book & Ukulele Basics*

I Want To Break Free *The Ukulele Playlist: Black Book*

I Wish *The Ukulele Playlist: Yellow Book*

I Wish It Could Be Christmas Every Day *The Ukulele Playlist: Christmas Book*

If I Had A Hammer *The Really Easy Uke Book*

If I Were A Rich Man *The Ukulele Playlist: Shows Book*

If You're Happy And You Know It *The Ukulele Playlist: Kids' Songs Book*

(I'm Gonna Be) 500 Miles *The Ukulele Playlist: Blue Book & Ukulele Basics*

I'm Gonna Sing *Ukulele Basics*

Impossible Dream, The *The Ukulele Playlist: Shows Book*

I'm Yours *The Ukulele Playlist: White Book*

In The Bleak Midwinter *The Ukulele Playlist: Christmas Book*

(Is This The Way To) Amarillo *The Ukulele Playlist: White Book & The Really Easy Uke Book & The Ukulele Playlist: Kids' Songs Book*

Is You Is, Or Is You Ain't My Baby *The Ukulele Playlist: Purple Book*

Islands In The Stream *The Ukulele Playlist: White Book*

Isn't She Lovely *The Ukulele Playlist: Blue Book*

It Had To Be You *The Ukulele Playlist: Purple Book*

It's A Hard Knock Life *The Ukulele Playlist: Green Book*

It's A Long Way To Tipperary *The Ukulele Playlist: Green Book*

I've Got My Love To Keep Me Warm *The Ukulele Playlist: Green Book*

JCB *The Ukulele Playlist: Orange Book*

Jean Genie, The *The Ukulele Playlist: Black Book*

Jenny Don't Be Hasty *The Ukulele Playlist: White Book*

Jingle Bells *The Ukulele Playlist: Christmas Book*

Jive Talkin' *The Ukulele Playlist: Red Book*

Joy To The World *The Ukulele Playlist: Christmas Book*

Karma Chameleon *The Ukulele Playlist: Red Book*

Kids In America *The Ukulele Playlist: Blue Book*

King Of The Road *The Ukulele Playlist: Yellow Book*

Kiss Me *The Ukulele Playlist: Orange Book*

Knees Up Mother Brown *The Really Easy Uke Book*

Kum-Ba-Yah *The Really Easy Uke Book*

Ku-U-I-Po *The Ukulele Playlist: Green Book*

Last Christmas *The Ukulele Playlist: Christmas Book*

Last Nite *The Ukulele Playlist: Blue Book & The Ukulele Playlist: Black Book*

Let There Be Love *The Ukulele Playlist: Purple Book*

Let's Call The Whole Thing Off *The Ukulele Playlist: Purple Book*

Let's Do It (Let's Fall In Love) *The Ukulele Playlist: Shows Book*

Let's Face The Music And Dance *The Ukulele Playlist: Purple Book*

Let's Go Fly A Kite *The Ukulele Playlist: Kids' Songs Book*

Life On Mars? *The Ukulele Playlist: Yellow Book*

Like A Prayer *The Ukulele Playlist: Yellow Book*

Lithium *The Ukulele Playlist: Black Book*

Little Brown Jug *The Really Easy Uke Book*

Little Drummer Boy, The *The Ukulele Playlist: Christmas Book*

Live And Let Die *The Ukulele Playlist: Black Book*

Living Doll *The Ukulele Playlist: White Book*

Look Of Love, The *The Ukulele Playlist: Purple Book*

Losing My Mind *The Ukulele Playlist: Shows Book*

Losing My Religion *The Ukulele Playlist: Yellow Book*

Love Changes Everything *The Ukulele Playlist: Shows Book*

Love Is A Losing Game *The Ukulele Playlist: Red Book*

Love Is In The Air *The Ukulele Playlist: Orange Book*

Love Machine *The Ukulele Playlist: Orange Book*

Lucky *The Ukulele Playlist: Black Book*

Lullaby Of Birdland *The Ukulele Playlist: Purple Book*

Mack The Knife *The Ukulele Playlist: Red Book*

Mad About The Boy *The Ukulele Playlist: Purple Book*

Making Plans For Nigel *The Ukulele Playlist: Red Book*

Mamma Mia *The Ukulele Playlist: Yellow Book*

Man Who Sold The World, The *The Ukulele Playlist: Blue Book*

Material Girl *The Ukulele Playlist: White Book*

Maybe This Time *The Ukulele Playlist: Shows Book*

(Meet) The Flintstones *The Ukulele Playlist: Kids' Songs Book*

Memory *The Ukulele Playlist: Shows Book*

Merry Christmas Everyone *The Ukulele Playlist: Christmas Book*

Merry Xmas Everybody *The Ukulele Playlist: Christmas Book*

Mmmbop *The Ukulele Playlist: Red Book*

Monster *The Ukulele Playlist: Black Book*

Monster Mash *The Ukulele Playlist: Kids' Songs Book*

Moondance *The Ukulele Playlist: Purple Book*

More Than A Woman *The Ukulele Playlist: Orange Book*

My Baby Just Cares For Me *The Ukulele Playlist: White Book & The Ukulele Playlist: Purple Book*

My Funny Valentine *The Ukulele Playlist: Purple Book*

My Girl *The Ukulele Playlist: Red Book*

My Grandfather's Clock *The Really Easy Uke Book & The Ukulele Playlist: Kids' Songs Book*

My Old Man's A Dustman *The Ukulele Playlist: Kids' Songs Book*

My Sharona *The Ukulele Playlist: Black Book*

My Way *The Ukulele Playlist: Red Book*

Never Want To Say It's Love *The Ukulele Playlist: Blue Book*

No Surprises *The Ukulele Playlist: Red Book*

Nutbush City Limits *The Ukulele Playlist: Blue Book*

O Come All Ye Faithful *The Ukulele Playlist: Christmas Book*

Oh Dear, What Can The Matter Be *The Ukulele Playlist: Kids' Songs Book*

O Holy Night *The Ukulele Playlist: Christmas Book*

Oh, What A Beautiful Morning *The Ukulele Playlist: Shows Book*

Old King Cole *The Ukulele Playlist: Kids' Songs Book*

Old MacDonald *The Ukulele Playlist: Kids' Songs Book*

On The Street Where You Live *The Ukulele Playlist: Green Book & The Ukulele Playlist: Shows Book*

Oranges And Lemons *The Ukulele Playlist: Kids' Songs Book*

Over The Rainbow *The Really Easy Uke Book*

Panic *The Ukulele Playlist: Yellow Book*

Paranoid *The Ukulele Playlist: Yellow Book & The Ukulele Playlist: Black Book*

Passenger, The *The Ukulele Playlist: Blue Book*

Patience *The Ukulele Playlist: Orange Book*

Perfect Day *The Ukulele Playlist: White Book*

Please Don't Let Me Go *The Ukulele Playlist: Orange Book*

Postman Pat *The Ukulele Playlist: Kids' Songs Book*

Power Of Love, The *The Ukulele Playlist: Orange Book*

Price Tag *The Ukulele Playlist: Green Book*

Promise This *The Ukulele Playlist: Orange Book*

Proud Mary *The Really Easy Uke Book*

Raindrops Keep Falling On My Head *The Ukulele Playlist: White Book*

Razzle Dazzle *The Ukulele Playlist: Shows Book*

Real Wild Child (Wild One) *The Ukulele Playlist: Black Book*

Rebel Yell *The Ukulele Playlist: Black Book & The Ukulele Playlist: Red Book*

Rehab *The Ukulele Playlist: Yellow Book*

Rhythm Of Love *The Ukulele Playlist: Orange Book*

Ring Of Fire *The Ukulele Playlist: Yellow Book*

Rock Around The Clock *The Really Easy Uke Book*

To purchase any of these books, please visit your local music shop, or alternatively go to
www.fabermusicstore.com for a complete listing of our ukulele publications.

FABER **ff** MUSIC
fabermusic.com

A-Roving

Words and Music Traditional

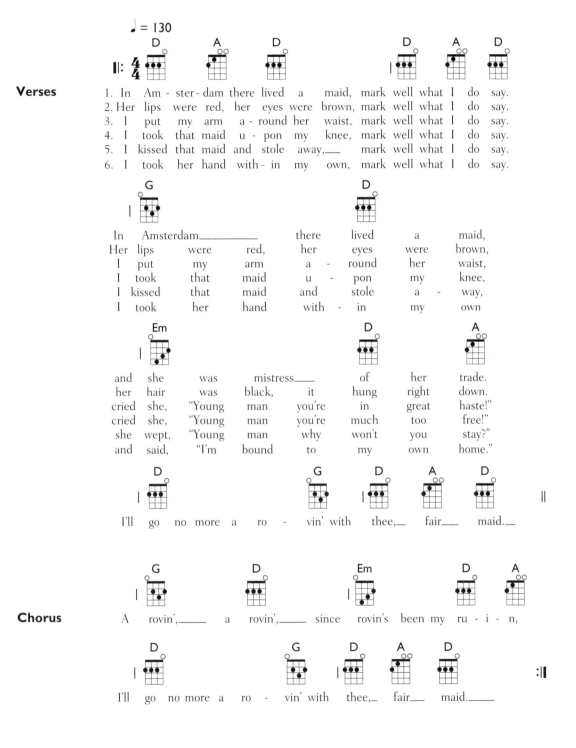

Verses

♩ = 130

| D | A | D | | D | A | D |

1. In Am - ster - dam there lived a maid, mark well what I do say.
2. Her lips were red, her eyes were brown, mark well what I do say.
3. I put my arm a - round her waist, mark well what I do say.
4. I took that maid u - pon my knee, mark well what I do say.
5. I kissed that maid and stole away,___ mark well what I do say.
6. I took her hand with - in my own, mark well what I do say.

G   D

In Amsterdam_____ there lived a maid,
Her lips were red, her eyes were brown,
I put my arm a - round her waist,
I took that maid u - pon my knee,
I kissed that maid and stole a - way,
I took her hand with - in my own

Em   D   A

and she was mistress___ of her trade.
her hair was black, it hung right down.
cried she, "Young man you're in great haste!"
cried she, "Young man you're much too free!"
she wept, "Young man why won't you stay?"
and said, "I'm bound to my own home."

D   G   D   A   D

I'll go no more a ro - vin' with thee,__ fair__ maid.__

Chorus

G   D   Em   D   A

A rovin',_____ a rovin',_____ since rovin's been my ru - i - n,

D   G   D   A   D

I'll go no more a ro - vin' with thee,_ fair__ maid._____

Rain And Snow

Words and Music Traditional
Arranged by John Renbourn, Danny Thompson,
Jacqui McShee, Terry Cox and Bert Jansch

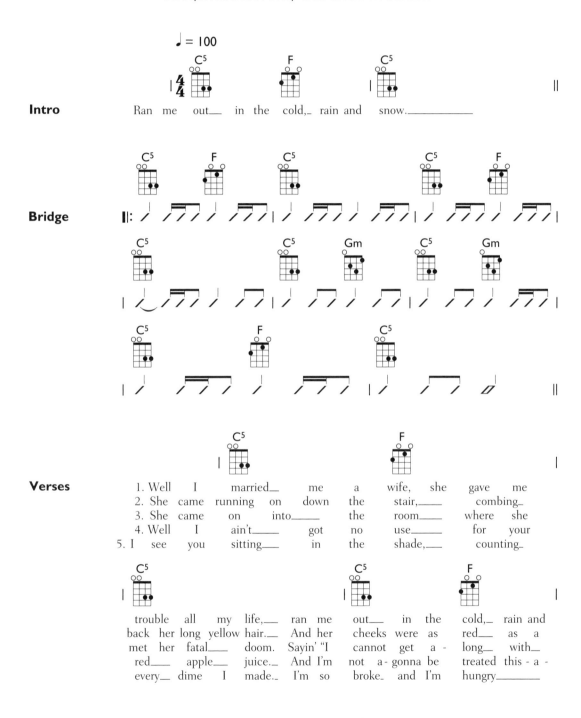

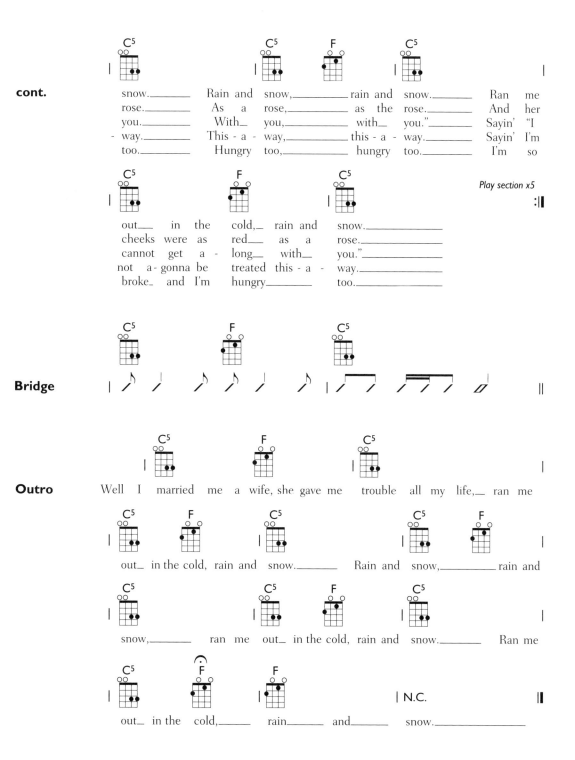

Reynardine

Words and Music Traditional

Verse

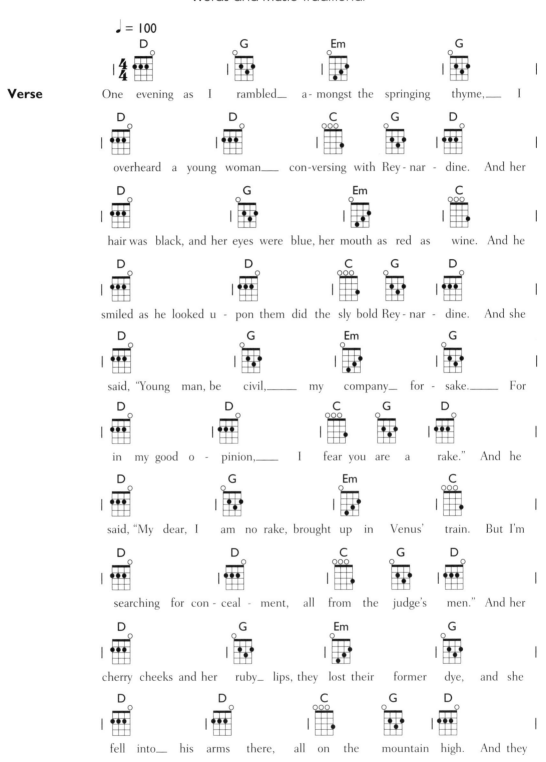

cont.

D	G	Em	C

hadn't kissed but once or twice till she came to a - gain. And

D	D	C	G	D

modestly__ she asked him,__ "Pray tell to me your name." "Well

D	G	Em	G

if by chance you ask for me, per - haps you'll not me find._____ I'll

D	D	C	G	D

be in my green castle,_____ en - quire for Rey - na - dine.". And it's

D	G	Em	C

day and night she followed him, his teeth so bright did shine, and he

D	D	C	G	D

led her over the mountain, did the sly bold Rey - nar - dine._____

The Rising Of The Moon

Words and Music by Traditional

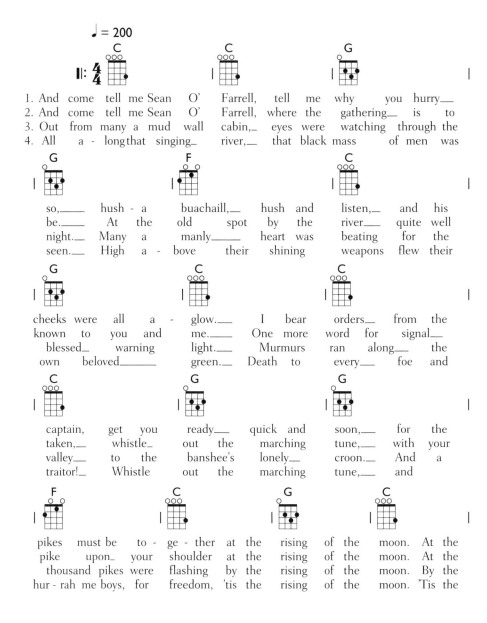

♩ = 200

Verses

| C | C | G |

1. And come tell me Sean O' Farrell, tell me why you hurry___
2. And come tell me Sean O' Farrell, where the gathering___ is to
3. Out from many a mud wall cabin,___ eyes were watching through the
4. All a - long that singing___ river,___ that black mass of men was

| G | F | C |

so,___ hush - a buachaill,___ hush and listen,___ and his
be.___ At the old spot by the river___ quite well
night.___ Many a manly___ heart was beating for the
seen.___ High a - bove their shining weapons flew their

| G | C | C |

cheeks were all a - glow.___ I bear orders___ from the
known to you and me.___ One more word for signal___
blessed___ warning light.___ Murmurs ran along___ the
own beloved___ green.___ Death to every___ foe and

| C | G | G |

captain, get you ready___ quick and soon,___ for the
taken,___ whistle___ out the marching tune,___ with your
valley___ to the banshee's lonely___ croon.___ And a
traitor!___ Whistle out the marching tune,___ and

| F | C | G | C |

pikes must be to - ge - ther at the rising of the moon. At the
pike upon___ your shoulder at the rising of the moon. At the
thousand pikes were flashing by the rising of the moon. By the
hur - rah me boys, for freedom, 'tis the rising of the moon. 'Tis the

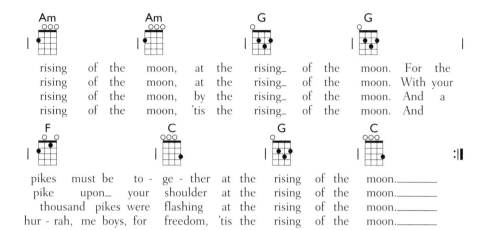

cont.

Am	Am	G	G
rising of the	moon, at the	rising_ of the	moon. For the
rising of the	moon, at the	rising_ of the	moon. With your
rising of the	moon, by the	rising_ of the	moon. And a
rising of the	moon, 'tis the	rising_ of the	moon. And

F	C	G	C
pikes must be to - ge - ther at the	rising of the	moon._____
pike upon_ your shoulder at the	rising of the	moon._____
thousand pikes were flashing at the	rising of the	moon._____
hur - rah, me boys, for freedom, 'tis the	rising of the	moon._____

Scarborough Fair

Words and Music Traditional

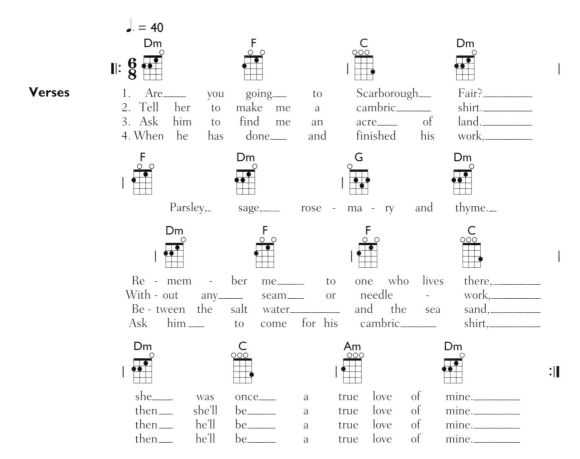

Verses

♩. = 40

Dm   **F**   **C**   **Dm**

1. Are____ you going____ to Scarborough____ Fair?_____
2. Tell her to make me a cambric_____ shirt._____
3. Ask him to find me an acre____ of land._____
4. When he has done____ and finished his work,_____

F   **Dm**   **G**   **Dm**

Parsley,_ sage,____ rose - ma - ry and thyme._

Dm   **F**   **F**   **C**

Re - mem - ber me____ to one who lives there,_____
With - out any____ seam____ or needle - work,_____
Be - tween the salt water_____ and the sea sand,_____
Ask him __ to come for his cambric_____ shirt,_____

Dm   **C**   **Am**   **Dm**

she____ was once____ a true love of mine._____
then__ she'll be____ a true love of mine._____
then__ he'll be____ a true love of mine._____
then__ he'll be____ a true love of mine._____

Shady Grove

Words and Music Traditional

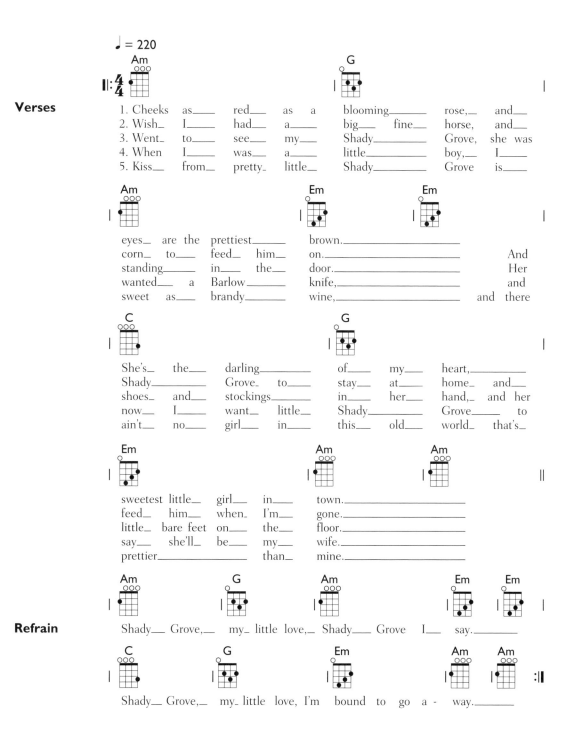

She Moved Through The Fair

Words and Music Traditional

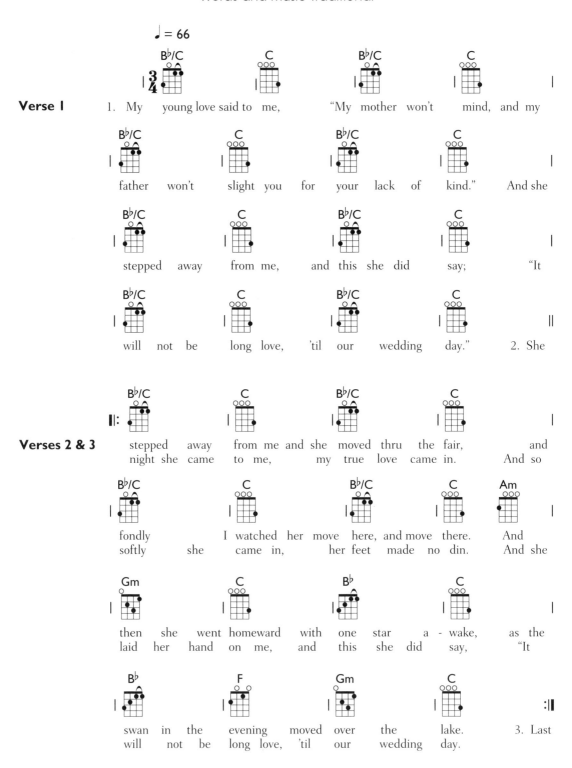

Verse 1

1. My young love said to me, "My mother won't mind, and my father won't slight you for your lack of kind." And she stepped away from me, and this she did say; "It will not be long love, 'til our wedding day." 2. She

Verses 2 & 3

stepped away from me and she moved thru the fair, and
night she came to me, my true love came in. And so

fondly I watched her move here, and move there. And
softly she came in, her feet made no din. And she

then she went homeward with one star a - wake, as the
laid her hand on me, and this she did say, "It

swan in the evening moved over the lake. 3. Last
will not be long love, 'til our wedding day.

Shenandoah

Words and Music Traditional

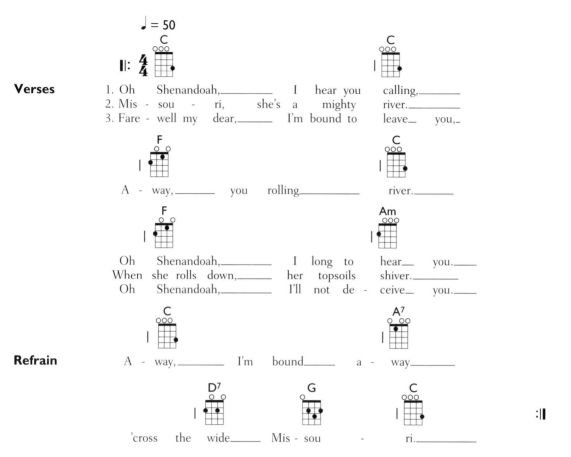

Verses

♩ = 50

C   C

1. Oh   Shenandoah,_____   I   hear you   calling,_____
2. Mis - sou - ri,   she's   a   mighty   river._____
3. Fare - well my   dear,_____   I'm bound to   leave__ you,_

F   C

A - way,_____   you   rolling_____   river._____

F   Am

Oh   Shenandoah,_____   I   long to   hear__ you.____
When   she rolls down,_____   her   topsoils   shiver._____
Oh   Shenandoah,_____   I'll   not de - ceive__ you.____

C   A⁷

Refrain

A - way,_____   I'm   bound_____   a - way_____

D⁷   G   C

'cross   the   wide_____ Mis - sou   -   ri._____

Siúil A Rún

Words and Music Traditional

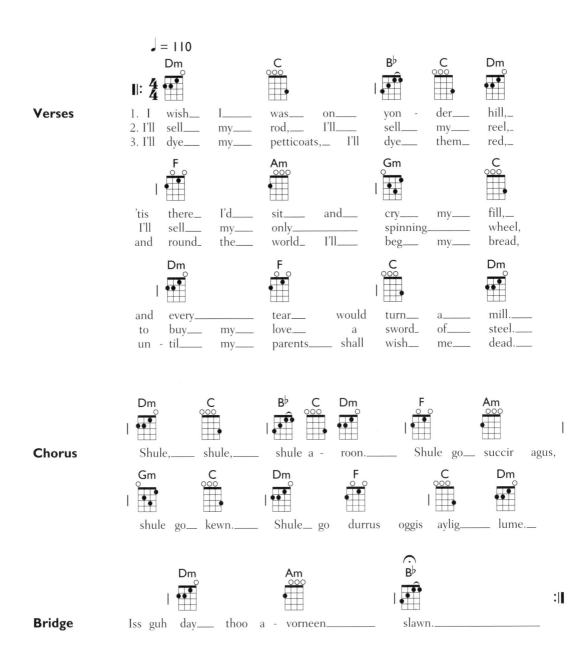

Verses

♩ = 110

Dm   C   B♭   C   Dm

1. I wish__ I____ was__ on____ yon - der____ hill,__
2. I'll sell__ my__ rod,__ I'll__ sell__ my__ reel,_
3. I'll dye__ my__ petticoats,_ I'll dye__ them_ red,_

F   Am   Gm   C

'tis there__ I'd__ sit____ and__ cry__ my__ fill,__
I'll sell__ my__ only_____ spinning_____ wheel,
and round_ the__ world_ I'll__ beg__ my__ bread,

Dm   F   C   Dm

and every_____ tear__ would turn__ a____ mill.____
to buy__ my__ love__ a sword_ of__ steel.__
un - til__ my__ parents____ shall wish__ me__ dead.__

Chorus

Dm   C   B♭ C Dm   F   Am

Shule,____ shule,____ shule a - roon.____ Shule go__ succir agus,

Gm   C   Dm   F   C   Dm

shule go__ kewn.____ Shule_ go durrus oggis aylig____ lume._

Bridge

Dm   Am   B♭

Iss guh day__ thoo a - vorneen_____ slawn._____

Skye Boat Song

Words and Music Traditional

♩ = 70

Chorus Speed bonnie boat, like a bird on the wing, onward, the sai - lors cry.

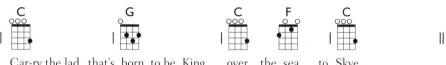

Car-ry the lad that's born to be King over the sea to Skye.

Verses
1. Loud the winds howl, loud the waves roar, thunderclaps rend the air.
2. Though the waves leap, soft shall ye sleep, ocean's a roy - al bed,
3. Many's the lad fought on that day, well the Claymore could wield,
4. Burned are their homes, exile and death, scatter the loy - al men.

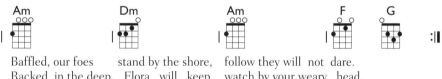

Baffled, our foes stand by the shore, follow they will not dare.
Racked in the deep, Flora will keep watch by your weary head.
When the night came, silently lay dead in Culloden's field.
Yet ere thesword cool in the sheath Charlie will come a - gain.

Spencer The Rover

Words and Music Traditional

♩ = 120

Verses

D   **D**

1. These words __ were __ com - posed_____ by____
2. In Yorkshire_____ near__ Rotherham,_____ he had
3. With the night__ fast__ ap - proach - ing,___ to the
4. 'Twas the fifth day of____ No - vem - ber__ I've__
5. And his children came__ a - round_ him__ with their

G   **A**   **A**

Spencer_____ the___ Rover._____
been__ on____ the___ ramble._____
woods_ he____ re - sor - ted._____
reason_ to____ re - mem - ber._____
prittle_ prattling_____ stories._____

D   **D**

Who travelled_____ most__ parts of Great
Weary_____ of____ travelling,_____ he____
With woodbine_____ and__ ivy,_____ his____
When first__ he ar - rived__ home_ to____ his____
With their prittle_ prattling_____ stories_____ which

G   **A**   **A**

Britain_____ and____ Wales._____
sat____ down__ to____ rest._____
bed____ for____ to____ make._____
family_____ and____ friends._____
drive__ care__ a - way._____

G   **D**

And he'd been__ much__ re - du - ced,___
At the foot__ of____ yon___ mountain_____
But he dreamt about_____ sighing,_____
And they did stand__ so____ as - toun - ded,___
And he's happy_____ as____ those__ as____

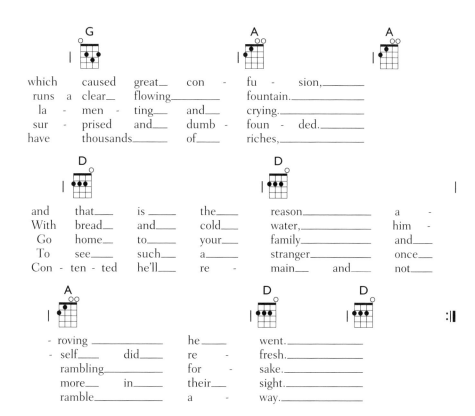

cont.

	G					A			A
which	caused	great__	con	-	fu	-	sion,_____		
runs	a	clear__	flowing_____		fountain._____				
la	-	men	-	ting__	and__	crying._____			
sur	-	prised	and__	dumb	-	foun	-	ded._____	
have		thousands_____	of__	riches,_____					

	D					D			
and	that__	is ____	the__	reason_____	a	-
With	bread__	and__	cold__	water,_____	him	-
Go	home__	to_____	your__	family_____	and__
To	see____	such__	a_____	stranger_____	once__
Con	- ten	- ted	he'll__	re	-	main__ and____	not____

	A					D		D	:||
- roving _____	he ____	went._____
- self____ did____	re	-	fresh._____
rambling_____	for	-	sake._____
more__ in_____	their__	sight._____
ramble_____	a	-	way._____

The Sun's Comin' Over The Hill

Words and Music by Karine Polwart

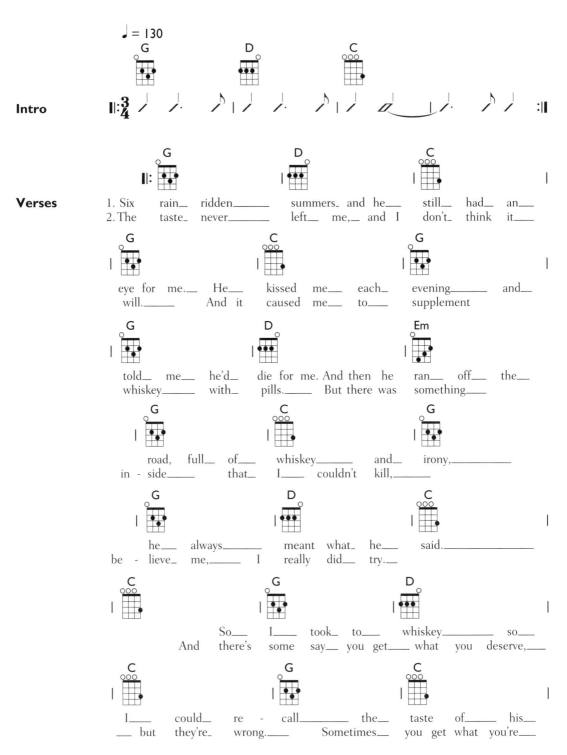

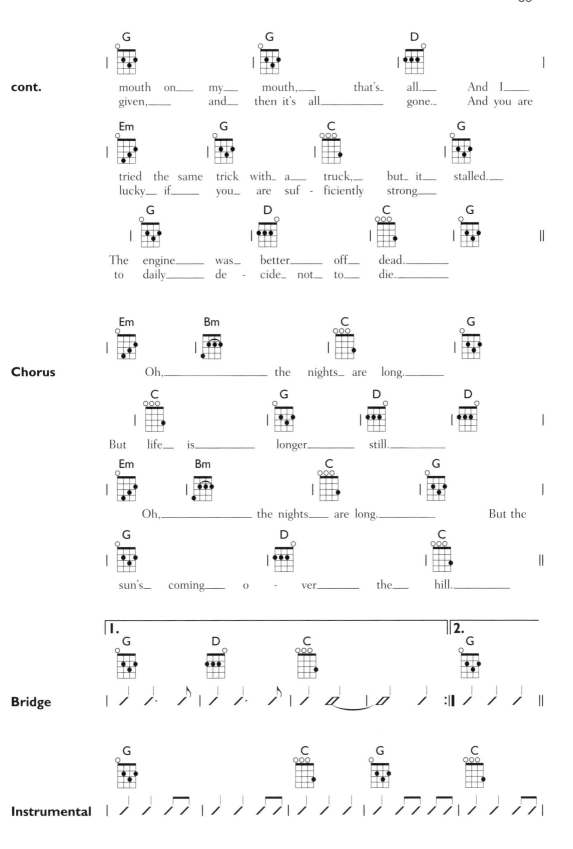

54

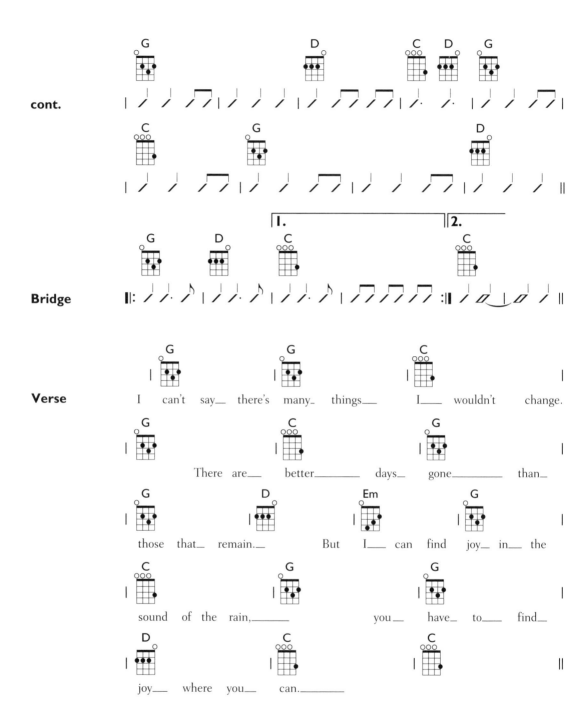

cont.

Bridge

Verse

I can't say— there's many— things— I— wouldn't change.

There are— better_____ days— gone_____ than—

those that— remain.— But I— can find joy— in— the

sound of the rain,_____ you — have— to— find—

joy— where you— can._____

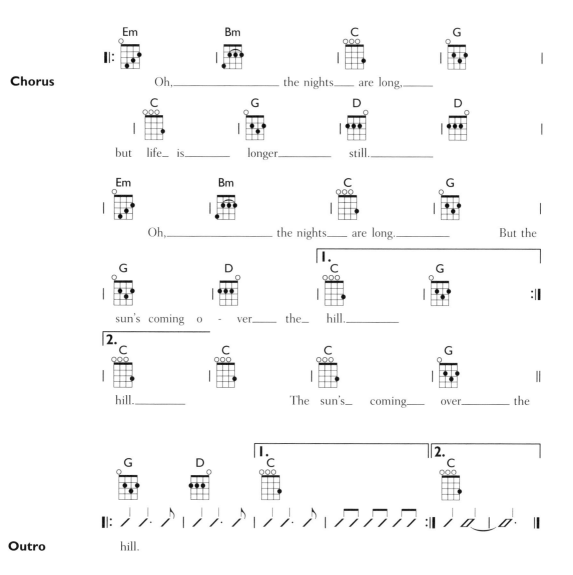

Chorus

Oh,_____ the nights___ are long,_____

but   life_ is_____   longer_____   still._____

Oh,_____ the nights___ are long._____   But the

sun's coming o - ver_____ the_ hill._____

hill._____   The sun's_ coming___ over_____ the

Outro   hill.

The Twa Sisters

Words and Music Traditional

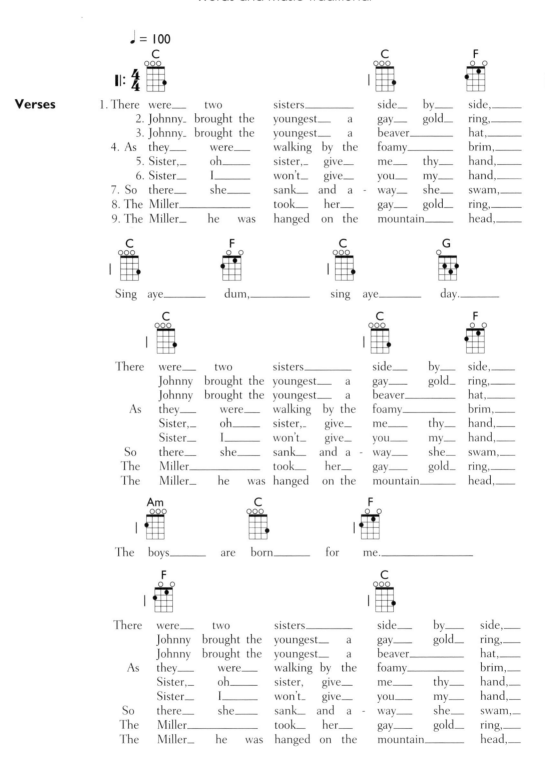

♩ = 100

Verses

1. There were___ two sisters_____ side__ by__ side,_____
2. Johnny_ brought the youngest___ a gay__ gold_ ring,_____
3. Johnny_ brought the youngest___ a beaver_____ hat,_____
4. As they___ were___ walking by the foamy_____ brim,_____
5. Sister,_ oh_____ sister,_ give_ me___ thy__ hand,_____
6. Sister__ I_____ won't_ give_ you___ my__ hand,_____
7. So there___ she_____ sank__ and a - way__ she__ swam,_____
8. The Miller_____ took__ her___ gay__ gold__ ring,_____
9. The Miller_ he was hanged on the mountain_____ head,_____

Sing aye_____ dum,_____ sing aye_____ day._____

There were___ two sisters_____ side__ by__ side,_____
Johnny brought the youngest___ a gay__ gold_ ring,_____
Johnny brought the youngest___ a beaver_____ hat,_____
As they___ were___ walking by the foamy_____ brim,_____
Sister,_ oh_____ sister,_ give_ me___ thy__ hand,_____
Sister__ I_____ won't_ give_ you___ my__ hand,_____
So there___ she_____ sank__ and a - way__ she_ swam,_____
The Miller_____ took__ her__ gay__ gold_ ring,_____
The Miller_ he was hanged on the mountain_____ head,_____

The boys_____ are born_____ for me._____

There were___ two sisters_____ side__ by___ side,__
Johnny brought the youngest___ a gay__ gold_ ring,__
Johnny brought the youngest___ a beaver_____ hat,__
As they___ were___ walking by the foamy_____ brim,__
Sister,_ oh_____ sister, give_ me___ thy__ hand,__
Sister__ I_____ won't_ give_ you___ my__ hand,__
So there___ she_____ sank_ and a - way__ she_ swam,__
The Miller_____ took__ her__ gay__ gold_ ring,__
The Miller_ he was hanged on the mountain_____ head,__

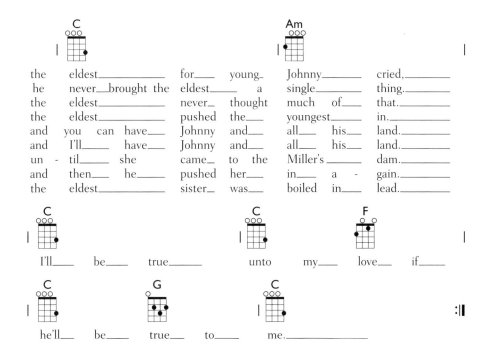

cont.

C	Am

the   eldest_____   for___   young_   Johnny_____   cried,_____
he   never__brought the   eldest_____   a   single_____   thing._____
the   eldest_____   never_   thought   much   of___   that._____
the   eldest_____   pushed   the___   youngest_____   in._____
and   you   can   have___   Johnny   and___   all___   his___   land._____
and   I'll_____   have___   Johnny   and___   all___   his___   land._____
un - til_____   she   came_   to   the   Miller's _____   dam._____
and   then___   he_____   pushed   her___   in___   a - gain._____
the   eldest_____   sister_   was___   boiled   in___   lead._____

C	C	F

I'll___   be___   true_____   unto   my___   love___   if___

C	G	C

he'll___   be____   true___   to____   me._____

:‖

Sweet England

Words and Music Traditional
Arranged by Jim Moray

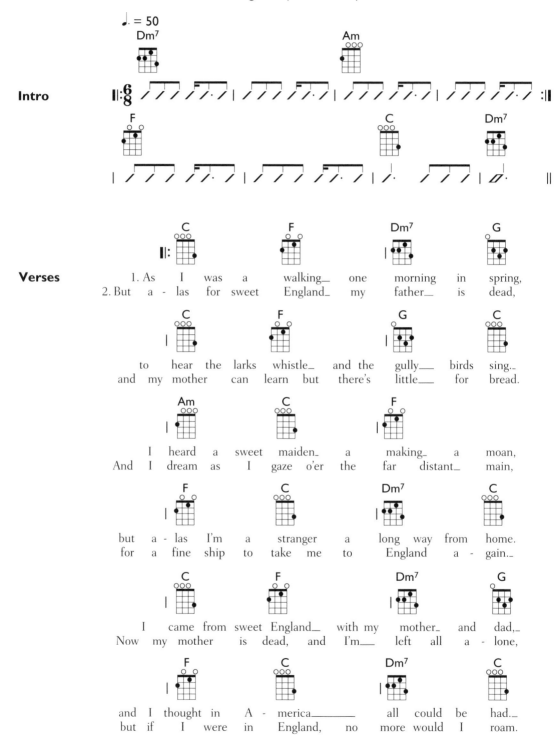

cont.

Am

Of   gold   and   of   silver___   and   acres___   ga - lore.
And the   aunt's   in   the   country,___   and she   loves   me   a - main.

Dm⁷   C   F

And I'll   never___   meet   hunger___   and   poverty_____
So   won't   some   ship   take   me   to   England_   a -

1.

Dm⁷   Am

⁶/₈ / / / / /. / | / / / / /. / | / / / / /. / | / / / / /. / |

Bridge   more.___

Dm⁷   F

| / / / / /. / | / / / / /. / | /. /. / / / / | /. /. :‖

2.

Dm⁷

| / / / / /. / | / / / / /. / | / / / / /. / | 𝅗𝅥. |

- gain?_____

F   G

Instrumental ‖: / / / / /. / | / / / / /. / |

Am   C   A♭

| / / / / /. / | / / / / /. / :‖ 𝅗𝅥.

Play section x3

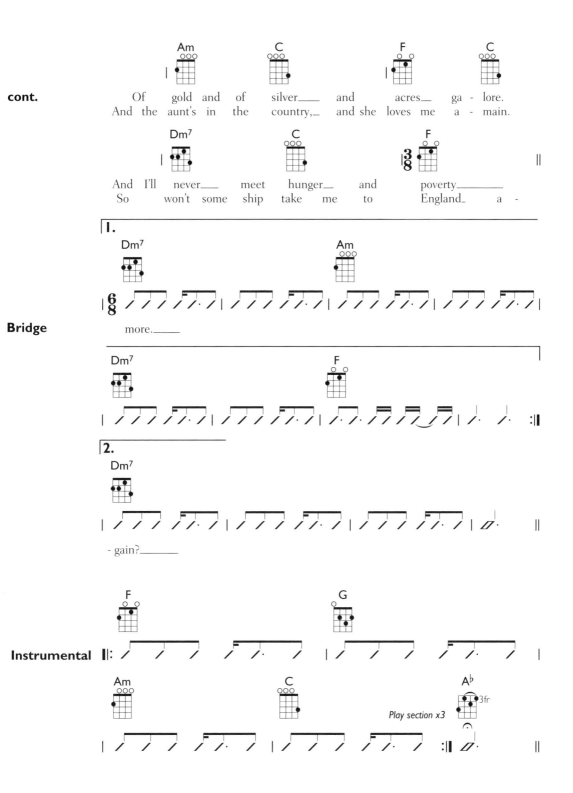

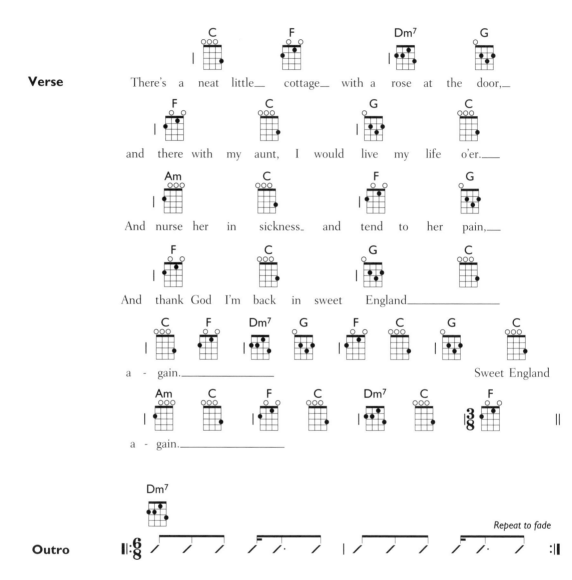

Verse

C · F · Dm⁷ · G
There's a neat little— cottage— with a rose at the door,—

F · C · G · C
and there with my aunt, I would live my life o'er.—

Am · C · F · G
And nurse her in sickness— and tend to her pain,—

F · C · G · C
And thank God I'm back in sweet England_____

C · F · Dm⁷ · G · F · C · G · C
a - gain._____ Sweet England

Am · C · F · C · Dm⁷ · C · F
a - gain._____

Outro

Dm⁷

‖: **6/8** / / / / /· / | / / / / /· / :‖

Repeat to fade

Waltzing Matilda

Words and Music Traditional

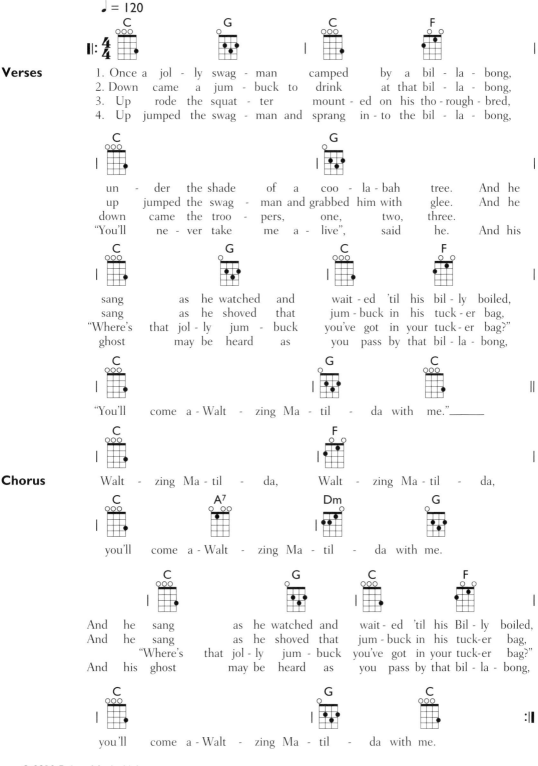

Verses

1. Once a jol - ly swag - man camped by a bil - la - bong,
2. Down came a jum - buck to drink at that bil - la - bong,
3. Up rode the squat - ter mount - ed on his tho - rough - bred,
4. Up jumped the swag - man and sprang in - to the bil - la - bong,

un - der the shade of a coo - la - bah tree. And he
up jumped the swag - man and grabbed him with glee. And he
down came the troo - pers, one, two, three.
"You'll ne - ver take me a - live", said he. And his

sang as he watched and wait - ed 'til his bil - ly boiled,
sang as he shoved that jum - buck in his tuck - er bag,
"Where's that jol - ly jum - buck you've got in your tuck - er bag?"
ghost may be heard as you pass by that bil - la - bong,

"You'll come a - Walt - zing Ma - til - da with me."_____

Chorus

Walt - zing Ma - til - da, Walt - zing Ma - til - da,

you'll come a - Walt - zing Ma - til - da with me.

And he sang as he watched and wait - ed 'til his Bil - ly boiled,
And he sang as he shoved that jum - buck in his tuck - er bag,
"Where's that jol - ly jum - buck you've got in your tuck-er bag?"
And his ghost may be heard as you pass by that bil - la - bong,

you'll come a - Walt - zing Ma - til - da with me.

The Water Is Wide

Words and Music Traditional

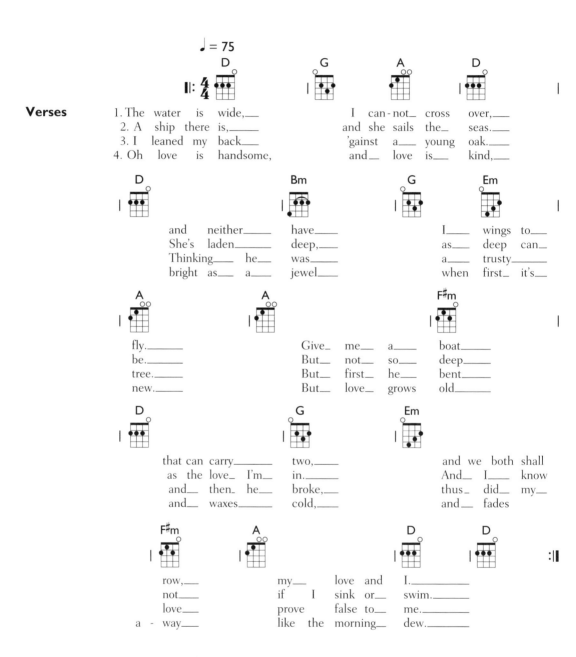

♩ = 75

Verses

1. The water is wide,___ I can-not_ cross over,___
2. A ship there is,___ and she sails the_ seas.___
3. I leaned my back___ 'gainst a_ young oak.___
4. Oh love is handsome, and_ love is_ kind,___

and neither___ have___ I___ wings to___
She's laden___ deep,___ as_ deep can___
Thinking___ he_ was___ a_ trusty___
bright as_ a_ jewel___ when first_ it's___

fly.___ Give_ me_ a___ boat___
be.___ But_ not_ so___ deep___
tree.___ But_ first_ he_ bent___
new.___ But_ love_ grows old___

that can carry___ two,___ and we both shall
as the love_ I'm_ in.___ And_ I___ know
and_ then_ he_ broke,___ thus_ did_ my_
and_ waxes___ cold,___ and_ fades

row,___ my_ love and I.___
not___ if I sink or_ swim.___
love___ prove false to_ me.___
a - way___ like the morning_ dew.___

Way Over Yonder In The Minor Key

Words by Woody Guthrie
Music by Billy Bragg

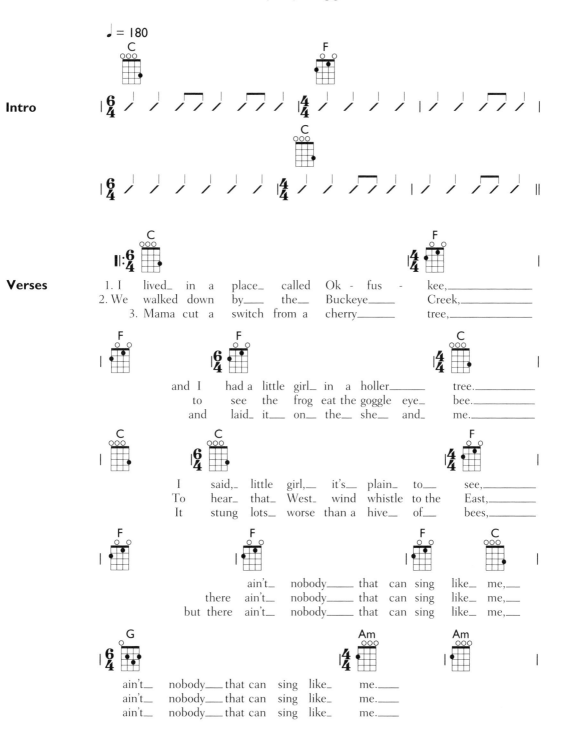

cont.

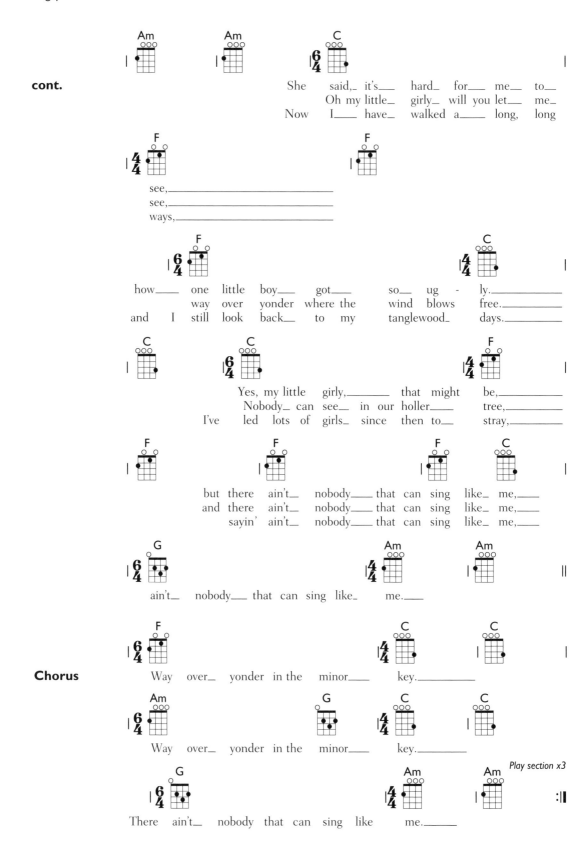

Am   Am   C

She   said,_ it's__ hard_ for__ me_ to__
Oh my little_ girly_ will you let__ me__
Now   I___ have_ walked a____ long, long

F   F

see,_____
see,_____
ways,_____

F   C

how____ one little boy___ got___   so__ ug - ly._____
way over yonder where the   wind blows   free._____
and   I   still look back__ to my   tanglewood_ days._____

C   C   F

Yes, my little girly,_____ that might   be,_____
Nobody_ can see__ in our holler____   tree,_____
I've   led lots of girls_ since then to__   stray,_____

F   F   F   C

but there ain't__ nobody____ that can sing like_ me,___
and there ain't__ nobody____ that can sing like_ me,___
sayin' ain't__ nobody____ that can sing like_ me,___

G   Am   Am

ain't_ nobody__ that can sing like_   me.___

F   C   C

Chorus   Way   over_ yonder in the   minor____   key._____

Am   G   C   C

Way   over_ yonder in the   minor____   key._____

G   Am   Am

Play section x3

There   ain't__ nobody that can sing like   me._____

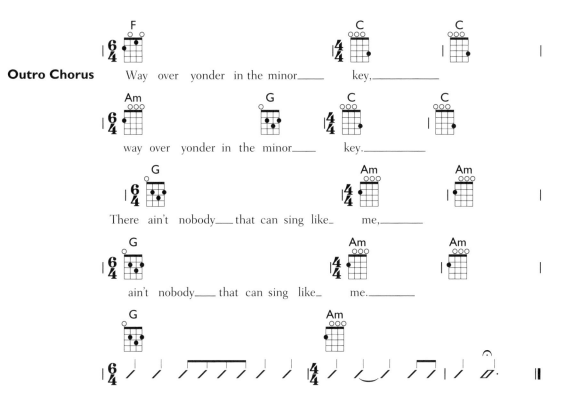

Outro Chorus Way over yonder in the minor____ key,_____

way over yonder in the minor____ key._____

There ain't nobody____that can sing like_ me,_____

ain't nobody____that can sing like_ me._____

Wayfaring Stranger

Words and Music Traditional

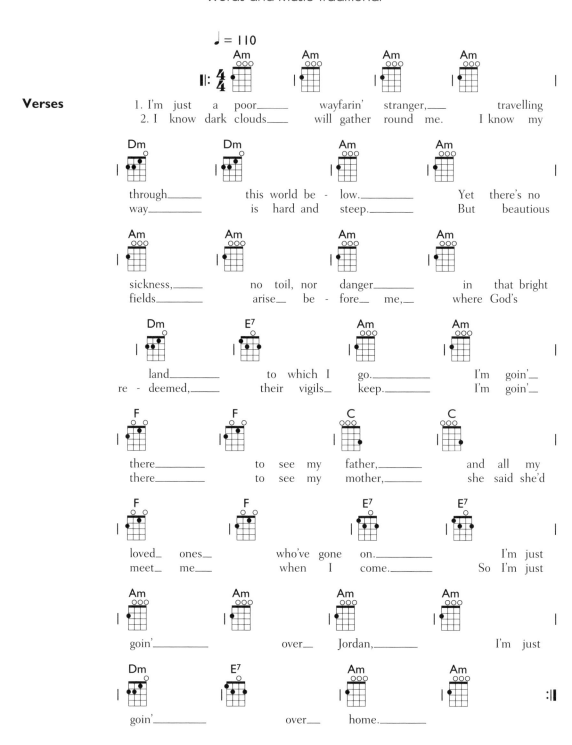

Verses

♩ = 110

1. I'm just a poor_____ wayfarin' stranger,_____ travelling
2. I know dark clouds_____ will gather round me. I know my

through_____ this world be - low._____ Yet there's no
way_____ is hard and steep._____ But beautious

sickness,_____ no toil, nor danger_____ in that bright
fields_____ arise__ be - fore__ me,__ where God's

land_____ to which I go._____ I'm goin'__
re - deemed,_____ their vigils__ keep._____ I'm goin'__

there_____ to see my father,_____ and all my
there_____ to see my mother,_____ she said she'd

loved_ ones__ who've gone on._____ I'm just
meet_ me__ when I come._____ So I'm just

goin'_____ over__ Jordan,_____ I'm just

goin'_____ over__ home._____

What Shall We Do With The Drunken Sailor?

Words and Music Traditional

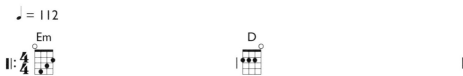

♩ = 112

Verses

What shall we do with a drunken sailor? What shall we do with a drunken sailor?
Put him in the long boat till he's sober, put him in the long boat till he's sober,
Shave his belly with a rusty razor, shave his belly with a rusty razor,
Put him in the scuppers with a hose pipe on him, put him in the scuppers with a hose pipe on him,
Pull out the plug and wet him all over, pull out the plug and wet him all over,
Lock him in the guard room till he's sober, lock him in the guard room till he's sober,
That's what we do with a drunken sailor, that's what we do with a drunken sailor,

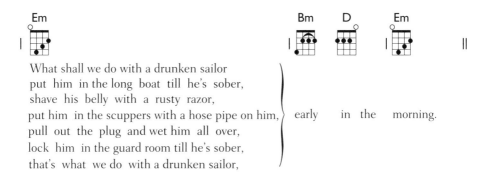

What shall we do with a drunken sailor
put him in the long boat till he's sober,
shave his belly with a rusty razor,
put him in the scuppers with a hose pipe on him,
pull out the plug and wet him all over,
lock him in the guard room till he's sober,
that's what we do with a drunken sailor,

early in the morning.

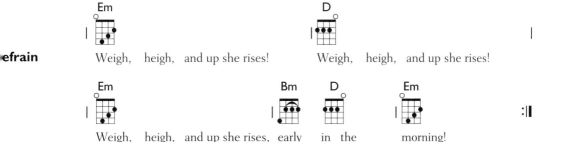

Refrain

Weigh, heigh, and up she rises! Weigh, heigh, and up she rises!

Weigh, heigh, and up she rises, early in the morning!

Where Have All The Flowers Gone?

Words and Music by Peter Seeger

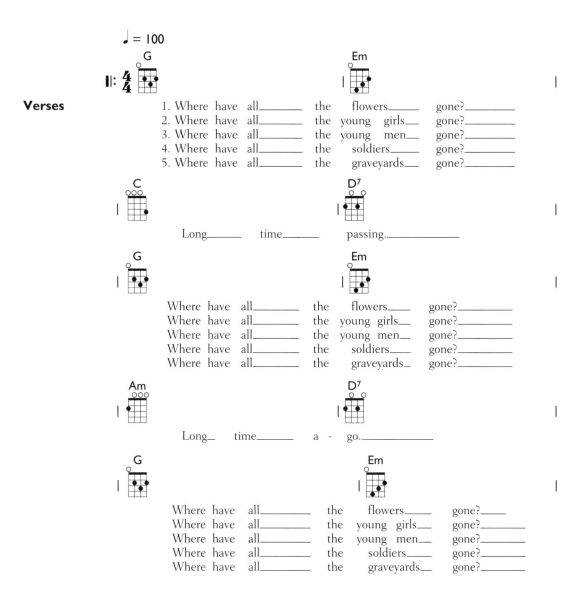

♩ = 100

Verses

G   Em

1. Where have all_____ the flowers_____ gone?_____
2. Where have all_____ the young girls__ gone?_____
3. Where have all_____ the young men__ gone?_____
4. Where have all_____ the soldiers_____ gone?_____
5. Where have all_____ the graveyards__ gone?_____

C   D7

Long_____ time_____ passing._____

G   Em

Where have all_____ the flowers_____ gone?_____
Where have all_____ the young girls__ gone?_____
Where have all_____ the young men__ gone?_____
Where have all_____ the soldiers_____ gone?_____
Where have all_____ the graveyards__ gone?_____

Am   D7

Long_ time_____ a - go._____

G   Em

Where have all_____ the flowers_____ gone?_____
Where have all_____ the young girls__ gone?_____
Where have all_____ the young men__ gone?_____
Where have all_____ the soldiers_____ gone?_____
Where have all_____ the graveyards__ gone?_____

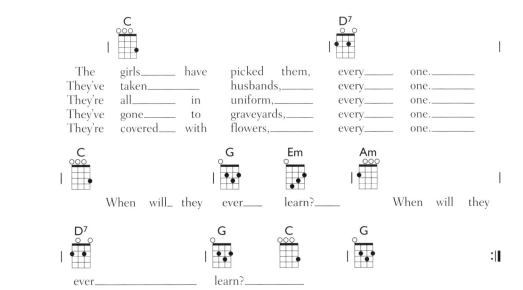

cont.

	C				D⁷		
The	girls____	have	picked	them,	every____	one._____
They've	taken_____		husbands,____		every____	one._____
They're	all_____	in	uniform,_____		every____	one._____
They've	gone____	to	graveyards,____		every____	one._____
They're	covered____	with	flowers,_____		every____	one._____

C

When will_ they ever____ learn?____ When will they

G   Em   Am

D⁷   G   C   G

ever_____ learn?_____

:‖

Whiskey In The Jar

Words and Music by Barney MacKenna, Ciaran Bourke, John Sheahan,
Luke Kelley and Ronnie Drew (professionally known as THE DUBLINERS)

♩ = 105

Verses

1. As   I was going   over   the   far famed   Kerry   mountains,   I
2. I   counted out his money and it made   a   pretty   penny,   I
3. I   went up to my chamber, all for to take a slumber,   I
4. 'Twas early in the morning, just before I rose to travel,   up

met with Captain Farrell and his   money   he was counting,   I
put it in me pocket,   and I took it home to Jenny.   She
dreamt of gold and jewels and for   sure it was no wonder,   but
comes a band of footmen and like - wise Captain Farrell.   I

first produced me pistol and I then produced me rapier, saying
sighed and she swore that she   never would deceive me, but the
Jenny drew me charges, and she filled them up with water,   then
first produced me pistol for she'd stolen away me rapier,   I

"Stand   and de - liver" for he were a bold deceiver.   ⎫
devil   take the women for they never can be easy.   ⎪
sent   for Captain Farrell to be ready for the slaughter. ⎬
couldn't shoot the water, so a prisoner I was taken.   ⎭

Chorus   Mu - sha   ring dumma doo damma daa.   Whack fall the daddy - O',

Whack fall the daddy - O', there's whiskey   in   the jar.

Verse 5:
Now there's some take delight in the carriages a rolling
And others take delight in the hurling and the bowling
But I take delight in the juice of the barley
And courting pretty fair maids in the morning bright and early

Verse 6:
If anyone can aid me 'tis my brother in the Army
If I can find his station in Cork or Killarney
And if he'll go with me, we'll go rovin' in Killkenny
And I'm sure he'll treat me better than my own a-sporting Jenny

Wild Mountain Thyme

Words and Music Traditional

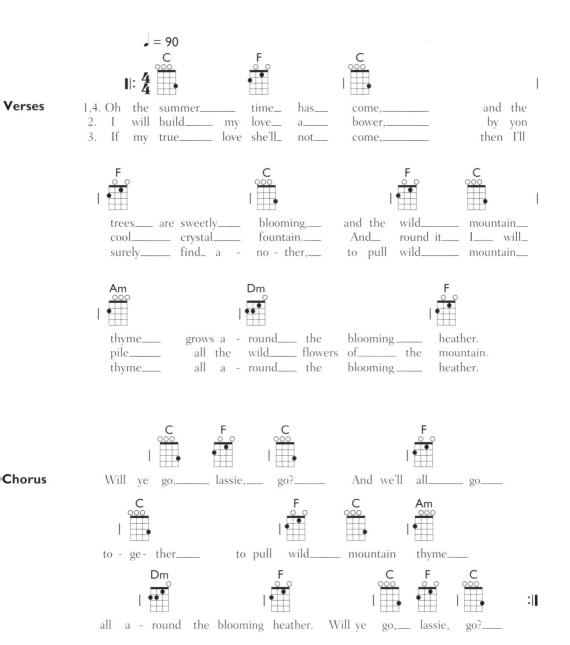

The Wild Rover

Words and Music Traditional

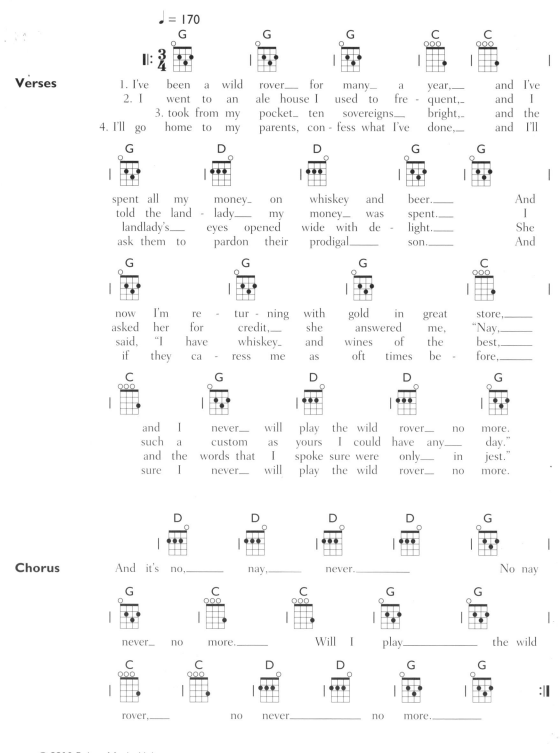

Verses

1. I've been a wild rover__ for many_ a year,__ and I've
2. I went to an ale house I used to fre - quent,_ and I
3. took from my pocket_ ten sovereigns__ bright,_ and the
4. I'll go home to my parents, con - fess what I've done,__ and I'll

spent all my money_ on whiskey and beer.____ And
told the land - lady__ my money_ was spent.____ I
landlady's__ eyes opened wide with de - light.____ She
ask them to pardon their prodigal_____ son.____ And

now I'm re - tur - ning with gold in great store,_____
asked her for credit,__ she answered me, "Nay,_____
said, "I have whiskey_ and wines of the best,_____
if they ca - ress me as oft times be - fore,_____

and I never__ will play the wild rover__ no more.
such a custom as yours I could have any__ day."
and the words that I spoke sure were only__ in jest."
sure I never__ will play the wild rover__ no more.

Chorus And it's no,_____ nay,_____ never._____ No nay

never_ no more._____ Will I play_____ the wild

rover,____ no never_____ no more._____